EMT CAREER STARTER

by Cheryl Hancock

LearningExpress ◆ New York

Copyright © 1998 Learning Express, LLC.

All rights reserved under International and Pan-American Copyright Conventions.
Published in the United States by LearningExpress, LLC, New York.

Library of Congress Cataloging-in-Publication Data

EMT career starter: finding and getting a great job.
    p. cm.
  ISBN 1–57685–113–3
    1.Emergency medical technicians—Vocational guidance.
  Emergency medical services—Study and teaching—United States—Directories.
RA645.5.E499   1998
610.69'53—dc21   98–6409
                           CIP

Printed in the United States of America
9 8 7 6 5 4 3 2 1
First Edition

Regarding the Information in this Book
Every effort has been made to ensure accuracy of directory information up until press time.
However, phone numbers and/or addresses are subject to change. Please contact the respective organization for the most recent information.

For Further Information
For information on LearningExpress, other LearningExpress products, or bulk sales, please
call or write to us at:
    LearningExpress™
    900 Broadway
    Suite 604
    New York, NY 10003
    212-995-2566

LearningExpress is an affiliated company of Random House, Inc.

ISBN 1-57685-113-3

7 85555 85113 9

ABOUT THE AUTHOR Cheryl Hancock is a freelance writer and editor based in Athens, Georgia, as well as a wife and a mother of two. She is also the author of a book entitled *Healthcare Career Starter*.

CONTENTS

INTRODUCTION

WHY BECOME AN EMT?

Becoming an Emergency Medical Technician (EMT) will put you in high demand. The career is currently growing at an excellent rate and is expected to grow up to 71% through the year 2005. There are half a million Emergency Medical Technicians today in the United States. You can increase your chances of landing this highly sought-after job by reading this book and applying its principles to your job search.

This book will give you the ins and outs on how to become an Emergency Medical Technician. Chapter one describes the duties of EMTs, the EMT work environment, the training EMTs need, and the certification requirements EMTs need before they can land a job. The chapter contains useful information such as specific job descriptions, typical salaries, and typical minimum requirements for each level of the EMT profession.

Chapter two tells you how to land the EMT job you want. It covers all you need to know about the many different aspects of the job application process, the written certification exam, the certification process, the job interview, and more. Also included are sample application forms, so you can practice filling them out. How to search for a job, networking, and how to use the Internet in your job search are all clearly explained. Several helpful Web sites are listed for your use. Competition for EMT jobs is keen, so you can benefit by getting armed with the inside information and advice in this chapter.

Chapter three contains information on training programs and a directory of close to 400 colleges and technical schools that offer various EMT courses. Course descriptions are included to help you decide what training program is right for you and how long you need to go to school for each one. The directory will give you a representative listing of schools across the country in order by city and state. All programs provide name, address, and phone number, so you can contact each school directly to get more information and application forms.

Chapter four contains detailed information on the financial aid process including sample financial aid forms, so you can practice filling them out. Several helpful checklists and tables are included for your use. This chapter also contains information on receiving funds through county, city, and state sources and tuition reimbursement (some EMS companies and hospitals will reimburse you for some or all costs of your education).

Once you've completed your training program and landed your first job, chapter five will reveal how to succeed on that job. You'll find out what qualities are rewarded by coworkers and supervisors, how to advance and move up in rank or title, and what specific advancement opportunities are available within the EMS field. You'll also find out what additional career options and areas of specialization are available to you as you progress along your career path.

Also provided at the end of each chapter are insider interviews that contain helpful advice and tips from professionals in the emergency medical services field from around the country who can give you the inside scoop on how to get hired.

So read on to find out how you can land a job as an EMT and succeed in this exciting, demanding, and heroic career.

CHAPTER | 1

This chapter is an up-to-date report from the field on the best opportunities in emergency medical services today from working for a private or hospital ambulance service to municipal employment with fire or police departments. Full-time, part-time, and volunteer positions are discussed, as well as the differences in the titles of EMT-Basic, EMT-Intermediate, and EMT-Paramedic and the certification procedures required for each. This chapter gives you hiring statistics, starting salaries, benefits, job descriptions, work conditions, and checklists and evaluation examples to help you find out if this job is for you.

ALL ABOUT EMTS

Have you ever considered working in an unpredictable and challenging field where you can help people and maybe even save someone's life? You can do this and more with a career in the emergency medical services.

If you've ever been involved in any type of accident or crisis situation, you may have been in need of emergency services. Anyone who has ever been helped by an Emergency Medical Technician (EMT) who responded to his or her accident knows how important this emergency specialist really is. Emergency Medical Technicians aid and save millions of lives each year.

Emergency Medical Technicians, often referred to as EMTs, are those people who respond to medical emergencies, especially 911 calls, to provide immediate treatment for sick or injured persons both on the scene of an accident and during ambulance transport to a medical facility. There are half a million practicing EMTs in the United States today. These technicians are the first care providers to arrive at the scene of an accident, and their adequate assessment of treatment is crucial to the life of the victim. They function as part of an emergency medical team, and the range of medical and lifesaving services they perform varies according to their level of training.

Many people decide to become EMTs knowing how they may help another in a crisis situation. Some become EMTs after having been rescued by technicians. Theresa Sims, an EMT-Intermediate from Wilmington, Delaware explains:

> I became an EMT after having been rescued by one. I was riding too fast on my bicycle on a bicycle path on a resort island, trying to beat a storm that was coming. As I rounded a corner that was sheltered by some bushes, I suddenly saw a couple on bikes heading toward me too quickly to stop. I turned toward the grass when the woman's bike hit head-on into the side of my bike, and at the same time, her forehead hit me behind my left ear. The pain I felt was unbearable, like my head was splitting open. Luckily, someone went to the hotel across the street and dialed 911. The ambulance came, and the EMTs realized how badly I could've been hurt. I spent about 20 minutes with that team trying to keep me awake and talking to me, and then, when the local hospital didn't have a neurologist, I spent an hour with another team being transported to the next major city. I had a skull fracture and a sub-dural hematoma (blood clot below the skull), and from what they told me, I could've died. The time I spent with the EMTs made me think about what may have happened to me if they had not come to help me or to transport me to someone who could. That's when I decided I could return the favor to someone else some day, that EMTs must receive enormous satisfaction from helping those in need.

Whatever the reason, these dedicated professionals become the people who are critical to the survival of victims of emergency situations.

JOB OPPORTUNITIES FOR EMTS

There are many different job opportunities for EMTs—many more than the most widely known position of working for an ambulance service—and there are many different kinds of EMTs. EMTs can advance their careers with continuing education to work in even more wide-ranging positions as EMTs or in related career areas.

Volunteer EMTs

Volunteer EMTs are considered to be a rare breed of people. Volunteer EMTs can be found in both fire stations and private ambulance services. Many times, volunteer EMTs work in environments run by local governments of small, rural communities. Some people become volunteer EMTs to evaluate their interest in this occupation and then proceed to market themselves for a job opening. Others become volunteers because a company requested they volunteer before being hired full-time. As a first-time volunteer, you may be required to begin your career by running every or any call that comes in as a third person to gain as much experience as you can. You may not immediately get the hours you want or the respect you deserve.

Paid EMTs

Paid EMTs work for various employers and are paid for their experience and education. That is the main difference between paid EMTs and volunteer EMTs. More paid positions exist in larger, metropolitan cities like Atlanta, Dallas, or Phoenix where the turnover for EMTs is higher. The more rural the area, the more volunteer EMTs you will find. The following descriptions of EMT-Basic, EMT-Intermediate, EMT-Paramedic, Dispatcher, Firefighter, Police Officer, Air Transport, and career Armed Forces EMTs are the most common examples of paid EMT positions. More alternative career options are discussed in chapter five.

EMT-Basic

A majority of EMTs have only basic certification, which is known as EMT-Basic, or EMT-Ambulance. EMT-Basic training in most schools is 100 to 120 hours of classroom work plus 10 hours of internship in a hospital emergency room. Training is available in all 50 states and the District of Columbia, and is offered by police, fire, and health departments, in hospitals, and as a non-degree course in colleges and universities. See the section entitled *Certification* later in this chapter for specific guidelines on how to become certified as an EMT-Basic.

EMT-Basics can do such things as assess vital signs including pulse, blood pressure, and respiration; control bleeding; administer Cardio-Pulmonary Resuscitation (CPR); treat shock victims; immobilize fractures; apply bandages; splint fractures; treat and assist heart attack victims; and conduct emergency childbirth. Students learn to use and care for common emergency equipment, such as backboards, suction devices, oxygen delivery systems, and stretchers. The EMT-Basic course will also train you in dispatch language and terminology, so you can correspond with advanced dispatchers appropriately.

According to a 1995 study in the *Journal of Emergency Medical Services*, the EMT-Basic or EMT-Ambulance average starting salary is $19,919. They earn $33,962 annually working with the fire department, $22,500 annually working with hospitals, and $22,238 annually working with private ambulance services. The average wage is $26,333.

EMT-Intermediate

The second level of certification is called the EMT-Intermediate. People who obtain this level of certification can perform somewhat more advanced procedures, such as using defibrillators to give lifesaving shocks to a stopped heart, as well as other intensive care procedures. EMT-Intermediate training varies from state to state but includes 35 to 55 hours of additional instruction in patient assessment as well as the use of esophageal airways, intravenous fluids, and anti-shock garments. You must have successfully completed the EMT-Basic program to move to EMT-Intermediate, and you may only provide care in accordance with the level of your certificate. Refresher courses and continuing education are available for EMTs at all levels to aid in re-certification.

According to *the Journal of Emergency Medical Services* the EMT-Intermediate average starting salary was $21,818 in 1995. They earned $35,667 annually working with fire departments, $28,000 working with hospitals, and $23,330 annually working with private ambulance services with an average salary of $26,102.

EMT-Paramedic

A growing number of EMTs have attained the highest level of certification as registered EMT-Paramedics. This level of certification can be gained in an associate degree or certificate program. Training programs for EMT-Paramedics generally last between 750 and 2,000 hours and allow paramedics to give extensive pre-hospital care. Refresher courses and continuing education are available for EMTs at all levels to aid in re-certification. EMT-Paramedics are authorized to administer drugs intravenously or to operate complicated life-support equipment—for example, an electric device (automated external defibrillator) to shock a stopped heart into action. They can interpret electrocardiograms (EKGs) and perform endotracheal intubations. You must have successfully completed the EMT-Intermediate program to become an EMT-Paramedic.

According to the *Journal of Emergency Medical Services* the EMT-Paramedic's average starting salary in 1995 was $23,861. They earned $37,690 working with fire departments, $29,264 annually working with hospitals, and $28,619 annually working with private ambulance services. Their average salary was $31,137.

EMT Dispatchers

Police, fire, and ambulance dispatchers are usually EMTs as well as the first people the public speaks to when calling for emergency assistance. Dispatchers work in police and fire stations, hospitals, and centralized city communications centers. Usually, a 911 call will connect to a police department dispatcher first who handles the police calls and screens the others before transferring them to the appropriate emergency service.

When handling a call, dispatchers carefully question the caller to determine the type, seriousness, and location of the emergency. They then quickly decide on the kind and number of units needed, locate the closest and most suitable emergency service available, and send the team unit to the scene of the emergency. They keep in touch with the unit(s) until the emergency has been handled in case further instructions are needed. They may also stay in close contact with other service providers; for example; a police dispatcher would monitor the response of the fire department when there is a major fire or monitor an ambulance until it reaches a hospital. Dispatchers also stay in close contact with bystanders or family, and often give them lifesaving instructions while they await an ambulance or other emergency vehicle.

EMT dispatchers earn on average $29,454 if cross-trained and $24,695 working with fire departments, $20,637 working with hospitals, $20,327 working with private-for profit services, and $21,821 working with other government services with an average salary of $23,580.

Firefighter/EMTs

Firefighter/EMTs must be able to fight fires, rescue victims from a wrecked vehicle or burning house, and attend to victims until the ambulance service arrives. They respond to a variety of emergency situations in addition to fires. For example, they assist victims of natural disasters and spills of hazardous materials, and they provide emergency medical services to heart attack, stroke, and choking victims. They assess, manage, and administer treatment to ill or injured people on the way to hospitals or other medical facilities, most often in a life-support unit or an ambulance. Firefighters who are also EMTs are more useful to the community because they can provide the important service of attending to victims.

Firefighter/EMTs have daily chores they also perform around the fire house, but depending on the location, they may have more down time, or time spent waiting for calls to come in, than ambulance services that mostly transport patients. They may spend their down time training others, running rescue drills, learning to use a fire extinguisher or ax, taking continuing education classes, or pre-planning buildings for escape routes.

According to the Bureau of Labor Statistics, median weekly earnings for firefighting occupations were approximately $658 in 1996. The middle 50% earned between $513 and $832 weekly. Starting salaries earn less than or close to $387.

Police Officer/EMTs

Police officer/EMTs provide emergency victim support until an ambulance with additional EMTs arrives on the scene. The police officer/EMT mainly acts as a regular police officer who is constantly on patrol. He or she usually does not carry much equipment but is trained in CPR and may be able to shock someone back to life with a portable Automatic External Defibrillation unit (AED), which is usually carried with the police officer. These skills enable him or her to become the first responder to an incident.

Police officer/EMTs are also trained to comfort family members and victims, help control crowds and other bystanders, find locations in dark areas, control disorderly patients in dangerous situations, preserve evidence as appropriate, and lift and move patients, when necessary. Becoming an EMT while you are a police officer makes helping injured victims possible and you more valuable to your employers. This will almost certainly raise your annual salary as well.

If you are considering becoming a police officer/EMT and you are under 21 years of age, you can become an EMT-Basic or Intermediate and get some experience before applying to become a police officer. Twenty-one years or older is usually the minimum hiring age for most police departments.

According to the Bureau of Labor Statistics, the median annual salary for police officers in 1996 was $34,700. The middle annual salary ranged from about $25,700 to $45,300 with the highest at $58,500 or more. Starting salaries began at approximately $19,200 per year. You could expect a slightly higher salary for your training and experience as an EMT.

Automated External Defibrillator (AED)

AEDs are systems able to shock someone back to life, and they are portable so that early defibrillation is available to all levels of certified EMTs. Most EMT courses must include AED training; however, if it is not included in the standard training course, outside training is available. The use of AEDs is promoted throughout emergency medical facilities and used by all trained EMTs.

Air Medical Transport

Air transport EMT-Paramedics are trained paramedics who work in helicopters and airplanes, and they must meet specific requirements before working with air transport. They must have three years of experience as street EMT-Paramedics as well as Advanced Life Support (ALS) inter-facility transfers. Most programs also require current Advanced Cardiac Life Support (ACLS) certification as well as pediatric advanced life support. Pre-hospital trauma life support training, neo-natal resuscitation provider certification, and hazardous materials training all are pluses. Any other medical skills can help greatly to beat your competition.

These paramedics perform rapid transport from the scene of an accident to the nearest hospital or trauma center. Helicopters and airplanes routinely fly all types of critical care patients from one medical facility to another. People who need this service range from patients who may be unable to fly on commercial airlines to patients that may need to go across town, across the nation, or somewhere internationally in order to return home or to get the medical care they need. If you desire, you can also obtain a pilot's license and become an air medical transport pilot as well.

Armed Forces

If you're considering enlisting in the armed forces—the army, navy, air force, marines, or coast guard—to become an EMT or get trained in Pararescue, you should learn as much as you can about military life before making your decision.

Speak to friends and relatives who have military experience, and talk to a recruiter. Becoming an EMT within the armed forces can be a reality, but you will be required to enter into a legal enlistment contract first. This enlistment agreement usually involves a commitment of four to six to even eight years of service, depending on the branch in which you wish to serve. Two or more years may be spent on active duty and the rest in the reserves, depending on the terms of your contract.

Military bases need emergency medical services, air rescue, and fire protection just like civilian communities do. The main difference is that military bases employ people who are enlisted in that branch of the military or federal civilian personnel instead of relying on the municipal EMS, or fire departments. Since the job duties of military EMTs are similar to those of municipal EMTs, a job in the military offers good experience for someone who wants to apply for a municipal job after completing the military enlistment period. You may also go into the Reserves after completion of your contract with the military branch you serve.

Getting In

You can join the Armed Forces in high school under the ROTC branch and earn credit towards your career. Requirements for non-ROTC members include that you be between the ages of 17 and 27, a legal U.S. citizen or legal immigrant alien, in good health, drug free, and have a clean arrest record. If you are 17, you can join the armed forces with parental consent.

When you talk to a recruiter about joining whatever branch of the armed forces in which you are interested, find out if you can get a guarantee of being trained and placed in the emergency medical services field. If you achieve a high enough score on the skills tests and pass all other requirements, it may be guaranteed in writing that your career area will be within EMS as part of your enlistment agreement.

You will be required to take and pass the Armed Services Vocational Aptitude Battery test (ASVAB) prior to enlisting, which is like an entrance exam. After you are accepted into the military, you will need to complete 6 to 11 weeks of basic training and 10 to 20 weeks of additional technical school training to prepare for your career in the military. You may choose from a variety of educational programs, such as emergency medical care or pararescue training.

The Pay Scale

Salaries for military EMS, air transport, firefighter/EMTs, and pararescuers are on the same scale as for other military jobs. The level of salary you'll receive while in the military depends on the years of experience and the grade level or rank you have obtained. See the table below for a range of salaries in the military. The dollar amounts in the following table combine basic pay, the basic allowance for quarters, the basic allowance for subsistence and the average variable housing allowance. They also include the tax advantage from untaxed allowances. The figures do not include the average overseas housing allowance or the overseas cost-of-living allowance.

THE BENEFITS OF BECOMING AN EMT

There are many different kinds of benefits that are offered and which you will discover as an EMT. If you ask any EMT, he or she will be glad to describe a few. Most EMTs would begin by describing to you the personal benefits of providing such a necessary public service, such as saving someone's life or giving a spouse more time with loved ones. This EMT describes some personal benefits:

> After watching a child wait 45 minutes for an emergency team to come to the scene where she had been hit by a car, I and about 10 others decided that we could provide the service better. Of course, that was a time when EMS services were rare. Now I am a part of our local ambulance/fire services which includes three ambulances, two fire trucks, and a staff of 20 paid EMTs and 10 volunteer EMTs. The waiting period for a call in our town now is less than two minutes.

Other EMTs would describe the work environment as a benefit. Volunteer EMT Gwen Gray from Knightdale EMS in North Carolina describes what she sees as benefits to working with the EMS:

> We have paramedics provided by the county who are at the squads on a two-month rotating basis. I really enjoy meeting the different people who come through Knightdale. I have made some great friendships, enjoyed some fabulous gourmet meals, gotten new insight into other professions, and just had a wonderful time laughing with some of the best people in the world. I would trust them with my life (literally!). It's like having a second family you can depend on when you need them!

In addition to the personal benefits to becoming an EMT are the other benefits that are a part of the nature of the job and the benefits that are offered through employers. Of course, these benefits vary depending on the type of employer, but they generally include several or all of the following.

Work Schedule and Environment

Many people are drawn to the EMT field because they do not want to sit behind a desk in an office job and work 9 to 5 for five days a week. While work schedules vary for EMTs, among employers, they often differ from the strict 9-to-5 job schedule because emergencies occur all around the clock, not just during regular business hours. For EMT/firefighters, the work schedule often consists of 24 hours on duty followed by 48 or even 72 hours off duty or some other arrangement of significant time on and time off the job. Some EMT/firefighters use their days off to work outside jobs or conduct other business as a side income to supplement their salary.

In some geographic areas, each shift for EMTs may last from 8 to 14 hours, depending on if it's a day, night, or weekend shift. Even with shorter shifts and more routine work schedules, EMTs on these shifts still have a large variety of tasks, and they never know what the next emergency call will bring. While on duty, EMTs in less-busy departments may have small amounts of free time after the maintenance and training for their shift is finished to visit or eat until the next call comes in. However, many EMTs do not have any "down-time" since they are constantly going out on emergency calls or stocking supplies, cleaning equipment, or undergoing training. The level and intensity of the workload for EMTs varies among companies, locations, and population levels in their territory.

Employer Benefits

EMTs usually have a choice of health plans to select from their employer. These plans normally cover the EMT and his or her dependents. Life and disability insurance may also be provided. In addition, a certain number of paid holidays and vacation days, dental and vision insurance, and pension (retirement) plans are usually also offered by EMT employers. And some companies offer free life insurance and overtime pay for court duty.

A uniform allowance may also be offered as well as limited equipment allowances. Those EMTs who work for police and fire departments receive the same benefits as firefighters and police officers no matter what their EMT level status is.

Many EMTs would describe their salary as a benefit—they are receiving a salary for the opportunity to help others in need. The level of salary EMTs earn depends on the level of training and individual experience they have and type of employer they work for. Those working in the public sector, for police and fire departments, usually receive a higher wage than those in the private sector who work for ambulance companies and hospitals. Salary level also increases with increasing levels of skill and training.

TYPES OF EMPLOYERS

The total number of jobs for EMTs is expected to grow at least 71% or more throughout the year 2005. According to the *Journal of Emergency Medical Services*, EMTs held about 138,000 jobs 1994. Two-fifths were in private ambulance services, one-third were in municipal, police, or rescue squad departments, and one-fourth were in hospitals.

EMTs also work in industrial plants and other local organizations that provide pre-hospital emergency care. There are many different types of employers for EMTs.

Hospital Ambulance Services

The leading employer of EMTs is hospital ambulance services where a multitude of tasks exist from simple transport of hospital patients to responding to 911 calls to the scene of an emergency situation. Hospital ambulance services transfer many kinds of patients from home to the hospital or to home or a doctor's office. They also assist with neo-natal (baby) teams and cardiac technicians. When not on a call, these EMTs clean and stock ambulance rigs, perform other company duties, and may be called to help in the hospital emergency room. This is a great place to begin work as an EMT-Basic, where consistent routine will enable you to learn the EMT basics adequately.

Private Ambulance Services

There are also private ambulance services, which are not affiliated with hospitals and are usually funded or subsidized by the county, city, or volunteer organization for the community. Private ambulance services perform the same basic duties as the hospital service, such as transport of patients, and they are usually connected to the local area 911 system. In many cases, private services have less chores than hospital ambulance services, leaving the EMTs with more down time.

Fire Departments

Fire departments are becoming a leading employer of EMTs; however, these jobs require the EMTs to become firefighters as well. If he or she is the first responder to the scene of an accident, the EMT/firefighter can give emergency aid and medical attention limited to the equipment carried. Some fire stations have an ambulance whereas others do not. When there is no ambulance, limited medical equipment is carried inside the fire engine. These EMT/firefighters give immediate emergency first aid until further ambulance help arrives.

Police Departments

Many police departments are supporting their Police Officer/EMTs who are also certified as Automatic External Defibrillation unit (AED) carriers. These EMTs carry out the same duties as regular police officers but are able to give essential medical aid if they are first to respond to an accident scene. They will provide emergency first aid in the form of CPR or AED shock until other help arrives.

Industrial Plants

EMTs also work on staff or on call for industrial plants that may or may not be located far away from emergency services. Many times people become victims of the machines they operate, so having an EMT on site ensures that these victims have emergency care they would otherwise have to wait for. These EMTs do not have the same gear and may not have as much training as ambulance EMT workers, but they can tend to a victim until further help arrives, e.g., by giving CPR.

Air Medical Transport Facilities

Air medical transport facilities require the use of EMT-Paramedics. These units transport patients by helicopter and airplane from across town to across the seas. Air medical programs transport numerous pediatric patients, and many fly high-risk maternal patients. The volume of patients flown by the air medical transport industry should continue to grow, and this growth will create opportunities for the flight paramedic with a competitive edge.

Other EMT Employers

There are also other organizations such as *ski patrols* and *search and rescue units* that hire EMTs to provide aid in mountainous or snowy regions that require the aid of specially trained emergency service that may otherwise be unavailable. EMTs can also be found at *football games, concerts, parades, fairs, carnivals, amusement parks,* and other activity sites. The EMTs may be hired privately by the event organizer or hired from a local ambulance company to do a stand-by with one or two crews.

Lastly, there are the *Armed Forces* (army, navy, marines, air force, and coast guard), and the *American Red Cross.* To become an EMT within the military, you must first go to your local recruiter's office and discuss with a recruiter whether the armed forces is for you. Afterwards, there are several steps you must take, such as taking an aptitude test and a physical exam. The military offers financial aid for training courses and veteran's benefits to service personnel after completion of service. Some fire departments offer veteran's preference programs in which fire-fighters get extra points on their application exams for having served in active military duty. To join the Red Cross, all you need to do is volunteer. You can become a volunteer even if you don't have any training; however, you will not be able to advance without it. There are some paid positions within the Red Cross, but you must be certified and trained, and in many cases, they would rather you become a volunteer first.

WORK ENVIRONMENT AND JOB DUTIES

The majority of EMTs work outdoors in sometimes extreme weather conditions or within a victim's home. They also work under great duress having to use quick thinking skills and their own judgment to aid in critical and traumatic situations. EMTs must also work as a team to provide the best possible care to victims.

The goals of emergency medical technicians are to quickly identify the nature of the emergency, stabilize the patient's condition, and begin the proper procedures to help the victims at the scene and en route to a hospital. EMTs are sent out to emergencies in an ambulance by a dispatcher. The dispatcher acts as a communications channel and may also be trained as an EMT.

EMTs are often the first qualified aid-giving personnel to arrive at an emergency scene, so they must make the initial evaluation of the nature and extent of the victim's medical problem. The accuracy of this early assessment is crucial to the victim's recovery. The duties and capabilities of an emergency medical technician depend mostly on the amount of training they received. However, all EMTs are trained and qualified to:

- ♦ give cardiopulmonary resuscitation (CPR) to a person suffering cardiac arrest

- control the bleeding of a victim
- administer oxygen to someone who has stopped breathing
- deliver babies
- subdue a person's violent behavior
- treat allergic reactions
- apply splints and anti-shock suits
- treat wounds

Once on the scene, EMTs must be quick thinkers and cope immediately and effectively with whatever situation is awaiting them. They must be on the lookout for any clues, such as medical identification emblems, indicating that the victim has significant allergies, diabetes, a heart problem, epilepsy, or other conditions that may affect decisions about emergency treatment. Because people who have been involved with an emergency are sometimes very upset, EMTs often have to practice their skill in calming both victims and bystanders in a reassuring manner. They also must know what questions to ask bystanders or family members when more information is needed about the patient.

EMT-Intermediate Gary Anderson from Phoenix, Arizona describes the qualities an EMT should have to appropriately respond to an accident:

> An EMT must be a people person. By that I mean someone who cares for people, their feelings, and their struggle within an emergency situation. An EMT should also have a friendly and team-guided personality to be able to work with other EMTs or fire or police personnel on the scene. EMTs should be emotionally stable, level headed, have good flexibility, agility, and physical coordination and be able to lift and carry heavy loads. EMTs who work as firefighters must be physically fit to get victims out of dangerous situations such as wrecked cars or burning buildings. They also need good eyesight, especially when driving an ambulance at night.

EMTs who drive must be able to get to and from an emergency scene in any part of their community quickly and safely. For this they take required ambulance training courses. Many EMTs work in two person teams: one EMT drives, and the other monitors the patient's vital signs and gives whatever care is needed. For the protection of the public and themselves, EMT drivers must obey the traffic laws that apply to emergency vehicles. They must be familiar with the roads and any special conditions affecting the choice of route, such as traffic, weather-related problems, and road construction. When transporting patients to a medical facility, EMTs may use special equipment such as backboards to immobilize the patient before placing them on stretchers and securing them in the ambulance.

The choice of hospital or medical facility is not always decided by EMTs, but when it is, they must base the decision on their knowledge of the equipment and staffing needed by the patient. The receiving hospital's emergency department must be informed by radio, either directly or through the dispatcher, of details such as the number of people being transported and the nature of any medical problems. EMTs continue to monitor the patient(s) and administer care as directed by the medical professionals with whom they are maintaining radio contact. When necessary, EMTs also try to be sure that contact has been initiated with any utility companies, municipal repair crews, or other services that should be called to correct dangerous problems at the emergency scene, such as fallen power lines or tree limbs.

Once at the hospital or medical facility, EMTs help the staff bring the victim(s) into the emergency department and may assist with the first steps of in-hospital care. They supply whatever information they can about the victim's situation, verbally and in writing, for the hospital's records. In the case of a victim's death, the EMTs complete necessary procedures to ensure that the deceased's property is protected. Bill Boyd, paramedic and fire captain, explains caring for patient belongings:

> We carry patient belonging bags on our medic units. If we note something really expensive, we try to give it to a relative on the scene or take it to the hospital with us and turn it over to the hospital personnel. What we consider valuable may not necessarily be what the patient considers important; however, dentures are one of the biggest items misplaced, and they are not cheap to replace!

Once the patient has been delivered to the hospital, the EMTs must check in with their dispatchers and then return to their EMS site to prepare the vehicle for another emergency call. This includes replacing used linens and blankets; replenishing drug supplies, oxygen, and other equipment. They also need to send out equipment to be sterilized; and take inventory of the contents of the ambulance to assure completeness. At least once during the shift, they must also check the gas, oil, battery, siren, brakes, radio, and other systems of the vehicle. It is also imperative that EMTs arrive on time for shift changes to receive and exchange equipment with coworkers.

BECOMING AN EMT

There is a general path a prospective emergency medical technicians must complete before becoming an EMT. Here are general guidelines detailing how you can become an EMT:

Graduate from high school or obtain a GED

The first step to becoming an EMT is to graduate from high school or obtain its equivalency (GED), which can be obtained from most adult education centers in your area.

Conduct a self-evaluation

You should begin your career decision-making by creating a written profile of yourself, which is essential an evaluation of your abilities and personality traits. You can create this profile by jotting down on a piece of paper things that come to mind when you read the next section entitled *Evaluating Yourself.* Writing down answers to the questions in the next section is a good way to identify your strengths and weaknesses and discover whether you should commit to becoming an EMT.

Decide which training program best suits your need and then complete it

Research different schools for affordability and course length—see chapter three for more information about how to evaluate training programs and to find a list of schools in your area.

Conduct your job search

There are many different ways to search for work as an EMT and just as many different facilities. Conducting a successful job search is covered in chapter two.

Succeed on your first job

In chapter five, you will find out how to best succeed as an EMT in whatever EMS facility you find work.

Evaluating Yourself

Conducting a self-evaluation will help you discover whether you possess the qualifications and desire you need to become an EMT. You will begin to see your strengths and weaknesses guide you, so take this very seriously. An EMT describes some likes and dislikes about the job:

> I like being there when someone is needed. I don't really enjoy going on a call to a bad accident, especially since I have a teenager and know many kids around here. But, I know I can help get someone to a hospital and I love seeing them walk out of the hospital when their car looked like an accordian. I also don't get a lot of sleep when on duty. I'm usually too keyed up to sleep well, and I don't want to sleep through a call. This makes me tired the next day—especially when I have to go to my first job and work all day. Volunteers have regular jobs they have to go to no matter how many calls they ran with the EMS the night before or how few hours of sleep they had.

Begin your evaluation with how much *training* you wish to pursue and commit to; for example, an EMT-Basic certificate usually requires 6 months to one year of school depending on the type of program and if any extra courses, such as ambulance training, are taken. EMT-Paramedic training can take up to two years. Also, think about your area of interest and what you do well. What are the skills you most enjoy using? Identify what skills, gifts, and talents you have, and prioritize them in order of importance.

List all the *jobs* you've ever had including summer jobs, volunteer work, part-time jobs and any freelance or short-term assignments you've done. Then add a similar list of your hobbies and other activities including any special experiences you've had, such as baby-sitting or travel, or any other activities you enjoyed.

Do the same for your *education* listing the school(s) you attended, your major courses of study, grades, special awards or honors, courses you particularly enjoyed, and extracurricular activities in which you were involved.

Work environment is another key consideration in becoming an EMT. They work outdoors, under duress, and usually during traumatic situations. EMTs also must work as a team to do the most to save lives and clear dangerous situations.

An experienced counselor can be of great help in this decision process as well. Counselors can give you a series of vocational interest and aptitude tests, and they can interpret and explain the results. Vocational testing and counseling can be found in guidance departments of high schools, vocational schools, and colleges. Some local offices of the state employment services affiliated with the federal employment service offer free counseling. Counselors will not tell you what to do, but they can help guide you in your search for a specialization.

Evaluating yourself is important in defining the type of job you will be good at performing. Also, you can create a check-list of characteristics you may wish to fulfill, such as:

- ◆ Do you want to work with sometimes seriously ill patients?
- ◆ Do you want the chance to save someone's life?
- ◆ Could you handle sometimes terrible accidents and ugly situations?
- ◆ Can you work as a part of a team?
- ◆ Do you want good benefits and a challenging work atmosphere?
- ◆ Do you want a variety of tasks and situations?
- ◆ Do you want flexible hours, the night shift, or the 9-to-5 shift?
- ◆ What is your physical stamina or strength?

These questions can help you decide whether the job of EMT fits your particular circumstances. Keep adding specific things that appeal to you about the EMT job to the checklist as you read through this book. Some people become EMTs to evaluate their interest in health care and then decide to return to school and become registered nurses, physicians, or other healthcare workers. Robert Kagel, an assistant EMT chief, describes why he loves being an EMT:

> There is no one particular item concerning EMS that I can pin down that I enjoy the most. I just love it. It is a combination of the adrenaline rush, the element of the unknown, the people, the connections you make, the networking you do, the patients you help, the families you support in their time of need, and so much more. The camaraderie is the best of all. Many people say that they couldn't do my job…I think if you have a passion to help, more than likely, you can do my job. I use EMS as an escape. While I am heavily involved with it managerial-wise and clinical-wise, there is always an escape in it for me. It is my form of relaxation.

Advancement beyond the EMT-Paramedic level usually means leaving fieldwork. A career option for EMT-Paramedics is to become instructors themselves. An EMT-Paramedic can also become a supervisor, an operations manager, an administrative director, or an executive director of emergency services. They may also work in sales selling emergency equipment. These career options and more are discussed further in chapter five.

EMT Certification

In order to become an EMT-Basic, you must first meet the requirements for basic certification. EMTs who have graduated from the basic program and who have passed a written and practical examination administered by the state certifying agency or the National Registry of Emergency Medical Technicians earn the title of Registered EMT-Basic. In order to move further in your career, you must be certified again at each level and re-certified on average every two years. To be certified, you must have completed the required curriculum and clinical practice and pass a written examination.

In some states, the National Registry of Emergency Medical Technicians (NREMT) certification process is the only licensure process for EMTs. Other states have their own testing procedures. Some states offer new EMTs the choice of the National Registry examination or the state's own certification examination, and some may require both. A majority of states accept national registration in place of their own examination for EMTs who relocate there. Both the NR-EMT and state tests are based on the same curriculum, which is issued by the U.S. Department of Transportation, to ensure national standards for training, testing, and continuing education. Certification enables an employer to be sure that EMT candidates have the knowledge and skills to do their job at saving lives and preserving health.

There are several different texts available, and some based on the NR-EMT test, to help you study for the written certification examination. (A list of certification study booklets can be found in Appendix B.) Whether you will be taking a state test or the NR-EMT test, you will be learning and studying similar material.

There are minimum requirements you must meet before applying for certification:

- You must be at least 18 years old.
- You must have successfully completed a state approved National Standard EMT-B training program within the last two years.
- If your state does not require national certification, you must obtain official documentation of your current state's EMT-Basic certification.
- You must have successfully completed all sections of a state-approved EMT-B practical exam within the past 12 months. This exam must equal or exceed all the criteria established by the National Registry.
- You must complete the felony statement on the application and submit the required documentation.

♦ You must submit current CPR credentials from either the American Heart Association or the American Red Cross.

All 50 states have some kind of certification procedure, and in at least 31 states, registration with the National Registry of Emergency Medical Technicians is required at some or all levels of certification. An EMT cannot practice emergency medicine without the required certification.

EMT Working Conditions

EMTs must work under all kinds of conditions, both indoors and outdoors, and sometimes in very difficult circumstances. Regardless of extreme weather conditions and somewhat strenuous physical tasks such as lifting, climbing, and kneeling, technicians must be able to perform their job efficiently. They constantly deal with situations that many people would find upsetting and traumatic such as death, accidents, and serious injury.

Some EMTs work on rotating shifts, working a 24-hour shift for one to three days and then having two or three days off. Others work a single shift every day, totaling anywhere from 40 to more than 55 hours a week. Since emergency services are required on a 24-hour basis, night and weekend work is often required, and many technicians are on call for emergencies. Usually they must work irregular hours, including some holidays. Volunteer EMTs work much shorter hours, such as one or two nights or days a week depending on the quantity of calls received, and they may remain on call the rest of the time.

The working conditions can be highly stressful and emotionally exhausting, so many technicians find that they must have a high degree of commitment to their job. In spite of this, EMTs can receive enormous satisfaction from knowing that they are able to provide such an important and vital service to victims of sudden illness or accident. Ernie Paul, an EMT-Intermediate from Pasadena, California describes:

> I really enjoy being able to help others, but sometimes it gets rough. I think there is something definitely wrong with a person if what they see as an EMT at an accident scene does not bother them. Sometimes what I see and have to deal with makes me appreciate life more, and sometimes I wonder what is going on with the world. It takes a lot of dedication to perform emergency services for severe incidents, but it's rewarding on the other hand to help someone. They help balance each other.

Who:	Jeanine L. Hoffman
What:	EMT-Basic and Class Coordinator/ Primary Instructor
Where:	Hempfield Community Ambulance Association Landisville, Pennsylvania
How long:	Since September 1995
Degree:	High school; one year of college plus specialty training

Insider's Advice

I began in the health care field as a home-health aide. I felt I wasn't doing much as an aide. I helped people a little, washed and fed them, but then it was over. As an EMT, I found a way to try and really make a difference. I can go in and calm people down, make a hurt child stop crying and smile as I bandage him. I can give a wife her husband for a few hours more, or I can help someone having trouble breathing to breathe with ease. The public usually doesn't thank us—they usually don't realize we exist unless we are blocking traffic or helping them personally, but helping people makes it so worthwhile.

Insider's Take on the Future

I am currently a EMT-B and Class Co-Coordinator/Primary Instructor at Harrisburg Community College in Pennsylvania. I also work for Hempfield Community Ambulance Association as an EMT-B. Right now, I am waiting on the results to the NREMT-B test I took. The NR stands for Nationally Registered, which looks good on your resume and helps with transferring your qualifications to other states that are involved in the program (about 35 states work with National Registry right now). Pennsylvania only allows for EMT-B and EMT-Paramedic. I enjoy my current positions and am unsure where I may go next.

CHAPTER | 2

Competition for EMT jobs can be tough, so how do you come out a winner? This chapter will tell you how. You'll find statistics and information on the employment outlook for EMTs in various positions. Also included is information about the query letter, resume, and interview process, as well as the various methods for finding a job, such as searching help-wanted ads, using the Internet, and networking. Detailed information on the certification and application process for a range of EMT positions is covered, and sample applications are included. Plus, a variety of insider tips are added from current EMTs.

HOW TO LAND THE JOB YOU WANT

The best source for employment leads for recent graduates of the EMT-Basic program is the school or agency that provided the training. EMTs can also apply directly to local ambulance services, hospitals, fire and police departments, county and city offices, and private and public employment agencies. However, because new graduates may face stiff competition if they are seeking full-time paid positions, volunteering is always a positive option to finding an appropriate opening or to gain experience to prepare for certification. Volunteers are always needed, and you can apply to all the above named agencies or directly to the first aid squad in your community to become a volunteer.

As Dwaine Massey, an EMT-Intermediate/Fire officer from Athens, Georgia explains:

> I really didn't think about becoming a firefighter until a friend mentioned it. It sounded interesting, so I volunteered at the local county station for a while to find out if I liked it. When an opening came up, I took the appropriate application measures and became a firefighter. I wasn't sure about being an EMT. I had never thought about that either, but it became another facet of the job of fire fighting because fire stations require that an EMT be on duty. We are around accident victims that require immediate attention, and sometimes we are the first on the scene. I applied with the county, and when an EMT opening came up, I got in for training. The county paid for the courses and equipment, which was a great opportunity. I really enjoy my job, and knowing that I can help people even more makes a big difference. I'm still a firefighter, but now I am certified to give further aid when needed. If I had never volunteered, I wouldn't be where I am today.

Flexibility about the location of a job may help new EMTs gain a foothold on the career ladder. In some small, rural areas, salaried positions are hard to find because of a strong tradition of volunteer ambulance services. In larger and more populated areas the demand for EMTs is much greater, so if a technician is willing to relocate to an area where the demand is higher, such as a large city like Chicago or Los Angeles, he or she would have a better chance of finding employment. Also, some EMTs find themselves working at more than one ambulance service—they may work part time at two or more agencies.

HIRING TRENDS

The employment outlook for paid EMTs at the various levels is excellent, but it will also depend mostly on the community in which you are seeking employment. The total number of jobs for EMTs in the field is expected to grow at least 71% or more throughout the year 2005. As stated in chapter one, EMTs held about 138,000 jobs in 1994. According to the *Journal of Emergency Medical Services*, two-fifths were in private ambulance services, one-third were in municipal, police, or rescue squad departments, and one-fourth were in hospitals (Journal of Emergency Medical Services).

Many communities understand the importance of high-quality emergency medical services and are willing and able to raise tax dollars to support them. In these often larger communities, the employment outlook should remain favorable. Volunteer services are being phased out in these areas, and well-equipped emergency services operated by salaried EMTs are replacing them. However, in some communities, particularly smaller ones, the employment outlook is not as favorable. Maintaining a high-quality EMS delivery system can be expensive, and financial strains on local governments could hinder the growth of these services. In addition, cutbacks in federal aid to local communities and an overall national effort to harness medical spending may lead to reducing community-based health-related costs. Under these conditions, such communities may not be able to afford the level of emergency medical services that they would otherwise like to, and the employment prospects here may be limited to volunteers.

Another important factor affecting hiring trends is that as the population ages, the need for more emergency medical services should increase. The number of older people is increasing rapidly as is the need for more EMTs. Also, additional job openings will occur as more states build fire stations and hospitals, and begin to allow EMT-Paramedics to perform primary care on the scene without transporting the patient to a medical facility.

HOW TO GET CERTIFIED

The amount of time between completing your training program and meeting the certification requirements can be one to two years, depending on the state. If you allow too much time to pass, you could end up having to take the whole course again. Getting certified is just another part of becoming an EMT. EMT-Intermediate, David Saucer from Chicago, Illinois describes obtaining certification as, "the most stressful part of the job. I was so nervous during the test, I couldn't believe it. I wasn't half as nervous during my job interview."

When you have met all the requirements of your EMT program, you will be directed to contact the National Registry of Emergency Medical Technicians or your local state registry to obtain an application and find out where you can take the certification test. You may also find out that you need to make individual arrangements to take the exam in your state. The registration fee for the NR-EMT application is $15.

- There is a different certification exam for each level of EMT. When you contact the National Registry, you will find out whether the examination is administered through your state EMT office or whether you need to make individual arrangements to take the exam. The requirements of the examination are that you must:
- be 18 years of age or older
- have successfully completed, within the last two years, a state-approved EMT-Basic (or previous level) training program
- truthfully complete the felony statement
- submit current CPR credential
- submit a completed application
- pay the registration fee ($15.00 Basic, $35.00 Intermediate and Paramedic)

EMT-Basic Exam

The National Registry's EMT-Basic exam consists of two parts, the written and practical exams. The written exam is comprised of 150 multiple-choice questions. Exam content is based on tasks identified in the EMT-Basic Practical Analysis conducted by the NR-EMT. This analysis is the basis for the 1994 National Standard EMT-Basic Curriculum, which is studied in basic EMT courses. The written exam consists of six content areas:

1. Patient Assessment
2. Airway and breathing
3. Circulation
4. Musculoskeletal: behavioral, neurological, and environmental
5. Children and OB/GYN
6. EMS Systems: ethical, legal, communications, documentation, safety, and triage/transportation

The practical examination consists of several applications of emergency medical procedures. Section I requires verification of your CPR credentials from either the American Heart Association or the American Red Cross. Section II requires your EMT instructor to verify that you have shown a minimal level of competence in thirteen key skill areas. These skill areas include assessment and management of trauma and medical patients, cardiac arrest management, spinal immobilization, long bone splinting, bleeding control, and use of upper airway adjuncts and suction.

Section III requires you to submit proof that you have successfully completed a state-approved practical examination. At a minimum, the exam must evaluate your performance in these skills:

Station #1 – Patient Assessment/ Management Trauma

Station #2 – Patient Assessment/ Management Trauma

Station #3 – Cardiac Arrest Management/ AED

Station #4 – Spinal Immobilization (seated or supine patient)

Station #5 – Bag-Valve-Mask Apneic Patient with a Pulse

Station #6 – Random skill station. This will consist of one of the skills required in Section II.

EMT-Intermediate Exam

The National Registry's Intermediate exam consists of two parts, the written and practical examination. The written exam is made up of two parts. Part I is the EMT-Basic Reassessment of basic skills and knowledge. This part of the test asks 70 multiple-choice questions, which cover the material presented in the National Standard EMT-Basic Training Curriculum. Part II contains questions derived from the objectives of the National Standard EMT-Intermediate knowledge. This part of the test asks 80 multiple-choice questions covering: Roles and Responsibility; EMS Systems; Medical Legal Considerations; Medical Terminology; EMS Communications; General Patient Assessment and Initial Management; Airway Management and Ventilation; and Assessment and Management of Shock.

The practical section of the exam consists of five separate stations presented in a scenario-type format to simulate emergency situations that occur in a pre-hospital setting. The process is a formal verification of the candidate's "hands-on" abilities and knowledge, rather than a teaching, coaching, or remedial training session. The five stations are:

1. Patient Assessment/Management
2. Ventilation Management
3. Intravenous Therapy
4. Spinal Immobilization (Seated Patient)
5. Random Basic Skills

EMT-Paramedic Exam

The EMT-Paramedic written examination consists of 180 multiple-choice questions contained in six major parts based on tasks identified in the EMT-Paramedic Practice Analysis, which is conducted by the NR-EMT. The six parts are: Patient Assessment; Airway and Breathing; Circulation; Musculoskeletal, Behavioral, Neurological and Environmental; Children and OB/GYN; and EMS Systems, Ethical, Legal, Communications, Documentation, Safety, Triage and Transportation.

The practical examination consists of six separate stations presented in a scenario-type format to approximate the abilities of the EMT-Paramedic to function in the out-of-hospital setting. The process is a formal verification of the candidate's "hands-on" abilities and knowledge, rather than a teaching, coaching, or remedial training session. The six stations are: Patient Assessment/Management; Ventilatory Management; Cardiac Arrest Skills; IV and Medication Skills; Spinal Immobilization (Seated Patient); and Random Basic Skills.

There is a registration fee of $35.00 payable to the NR-EMT.

State vs. NR-EMT Exams

States may use their own written and practical skills exams, exams from the NR-EMT, or a combination of both. A state exam is usually quite similar to the NR-EMT's exam. The federal government mandates the curriculum of EMT courses nationwide. Since the exams are based on similar curricula, they are usually similar.

Should You Become an EMT?

If you are able to answer yes to most of these questions, you would make a good EMT.

____ Do you have the desire to help people in immediate need?

____ Are you patient and caring with people?

____ Are you skilled under extreme pressure?

____ Can you put others before yourself?

____ Can you work as part of a team?

____ Would you like good benefits and a challenging work atmosphere?

____ Do you want a variety of tasks and work situations?

____ Would you like the chance to save someone's life?

____ Are you physically fit, able to lift heavy things?

____ Are you mentally fit, able to remain under stress for a long period of time?

____ Would you be able to handle death and other terrible situations?

CONDUCTING YOUR JOB SEARCH

The more openings you can find, the better your chance of landing a job. Usually, people apply for many openings before they are finally accepted, and there are many places to look for these openings. Remember that your geographic location has a lot to do with the availability of jobs.

Help-Wanted Ads

Reading the classified ads of your local newspapers, trade journals, and professional magazines is a good way to find a job as an EMT. Job titles you should be looking for are those such as: Emergency Medical Technicians, EMTs, Emergency Medical Service, Ambulance Technician, Rescue Squad, Healthcare, EMT-B or EMT-A, EMT- I, and EMT-P or Paramedic. When you find a job posting that interests you, follow up on the ad by the method requested. You may be asked to phone, send a resume, or fill out an application. Record the date of your follow-up, and if you don't hear from the employer within two or three weeks, place another call or send a polite note asking whether the job is still open.

Help-wanted ads are found in many trade magazines and journals such as *EMT Magazine* and *The Journal of Emergency Medical Services*. Not only is this a good place to find advertisements, but the articles are an excellent way to keep up-to-date on current emergency medical trends.

On-line Resources

The Internet has become a great place to scout for jobs. There are multiple career centers on the Internet that have classified ads and specific career jobs available to qualified applicants. For example, at the http addresses, *www.careermosaic.com* and *www.jobweb.org*, there are job listings for EMTs.

There are also health and EMS magazines and journals on-line and Web pages of newsgroups that advertise jobs, such as *www.jems.com* (The Journal of Emergency Medical Services) and *www.medsearch.com*. Some hospitals and companies also have Web pages that list job openings, such as *www.medctr.ucla.edu/* (UCLA Medical Center) and *www.reidhosp.com* (Reid Hospital and Health Care Services in Richmond, Indiana). Use a search engine on the Internet with the search words "hospitals," "fire departments," and "ambulance centers," or search the name of a particular hospital or ambulance center to see if it has a Web site listed and classified ads. See the table entitled "Web Sites" for more job-related Web addresses.

> **Web Sites**
>
> http://www.careermosaic.com/cm – Jobs, company profiles, online job fairs.
>
> http://www.careerpath.com – Lists jobs from over 50 newspapers across the U. S.
>
> http://www.statejobs.com/employ.html – Focuses on jobs by state.
>
> http://www.hoovers.com – Company profiles.
>
> http://www.itellimatch.com – Online resources, resume creation assistance.
>
> http://www.jobbbankusa.com – The largest list of job openings on the Internet.
>
> http://www.monster.com – Over 55,000 jobs and resume assistance.
>
> http://www.occ.com/occ – Online resources, online job fairs, and career guidance.
>
> http://www.helpwantedpage.com – Job listings and company profiles.
>
> http://www.jobweb.com – Job listings, company profiles, and online resources.

NETWORKING YOUR WAY INTO A JOB

Networking may be the best and is sometimes the only way to find prospective EMT career opportunities. As Dwaine Massey mentioned previously, it opens doors you never thought were available and brings you closer to finding a job through a reference, which is sometimes better than searching on your own. Many times employers will hire you based on a current employee's suggestion because the employer respects the employee who recommends you highly. Do not leave networking out of your job search. Read on for some reasons why.

What is Networking?

Networking means calling and talking with friends, acquaintances, and people you don't know about jobs in your area of interest and for advice and support. If you would like to work as a firefighter EMT, get in touch with all the people you know who work in fire departments or who have friends or relatives in the field. Tell your family, friends, counselors, former employers, and anyone you know who may know someone you could contact about a job opening. You may discover a job even before the job opening is advertised.

Make a list of everyone you know in the Emergency Medical Services field. Send a friendly letter to everyone on the list. You might want to even include your resume to people who are in a position to help you, or you can call and ask people if they'd mind if you sent them a copy of your resume. Think about how you can begin making yourself more attractive to employers. Use your informal interviewing skills when you network with others.

You never know what opportunity someone will be able to find for you. Only about 20-30 percent of job vacancies are advertised since many employers look for employees by word of mouth. This is called the "hidden job market." In today's competitive climate, successful candidates must pursue all possible outlets. You want to gain as much exposure as possible. Steve Patts, an EMT-Basic from Phoenix, Arizona explains how networking helped him to enter a training program:

> To get into the EMT program at the closest school, I had to have a referral from a working EMT. I didn't know anyone who was an EMT, but my wife did. She has an uncle who works as a paramedic at a hospital ambulance service. She asked him if he could help me. He told me to come ride third on his ambulance team, where I would just watch and not help. I did, and he wrote me a referral just like that. I was in the program as soon as the next one started.

Gaining Good Contacts

When you're establishing a network, you need to consider all possible living, breathing human resources. Areas to draw from include family (parents, cousins, aunts, uncles, siblings), friends (neighbors and parents of classmates), school (teachers, counselors, administrators), previous employment (employers, coworkers, competitors), professionals (practicing EMT professionals in your field), and community (business people, clubs, associations, chamber of commerce, religious groups). You can also use magazine articles, newspapers, or other general publicity to begin targeting people you would like to include in your network.

Basically, anyone can be involved, and it is important not to overlook any possibilities. However, you shouldn't use a contact's name without permission because you may put your contact on the spot with an employer. Don't assume your friend will go out on a limb to recommend you. Once you have received the networking information, use your own ability to get the job.

Making Contact

You're ready to start asking others for help. This could be the most nerve-racking time, having to contact a whole list of people for favors and risk being patronized. However, the key to networking success and avoiding a major case of networking negativism lies in understanding that you aren't asking for a giant favor that creates a debt and gives others leverage over you. You are subtly empowering the other party while not asking for much in return.

The first thing you will do when contacting someone is identify yourself. If you are contacting a referral that someone gave you to contact, then you want to identify your referral source as well. Also, identify your background, motives, objectives, and your reason for calling. This should get the contact familiar enough with who you are and why you are calling or writing.

Your contacts' willingness to help you will depend largely on how your requests are formed. Keep your requests for help brief, conversational, and low-key. Be sincere in your use of words.

- Ask contacts if they have time to talk for about 10 minutes, and then ask for their help in sharing with you any information they may have about openings pertinent to your job goals.
- Say you don't expect an immediate answer, and ask if you could call them back or meet at a specific date and time.
- Use phrases such as, "if I could make an appointment to talk" or "if we could meet for a few minutes so that I might get your thoughts and opinions about some job search ideas I've been thinking about" or "if I could drop in on you at work for a few minutes and pick your brain" or "if I could get some advice on getting some exposure in the emergency medical services market."
- Keep it light and pleasant, and to make it all easier, recite what you plan to say before you actually make that important call.
- Last, but certainly not least, thank the people you called or wrote for their time in speaking with you or time in attention to your letter. Tell them how much you appreciate their help and that you are grateful for their willingness to mention you to their colleagues. Thank them as well for any referrals they may have given you. If they gave you a referral, they must think highly of you. Let them know also that you will keep them posted on where things go from here. Most contacts will be interested to know that their input actually helped you.

Expanding Your Contacts

Ask the people you contact for other contacts too. These are called referrals. Your contacts may want to call the referral themselves to prepare the person and to find out if she or he minds becoming a contact for you.

Don't be afraid to contact people directly, even if they are complete strangers to you. You are actually paying them a compliment by contacting them. People like to talk about themselves. And remember, everybody likes a good listener—especially when they're giving their personal advice, information, and wisdom.

Organizing Your Contact List

You may decide to use a Rolodex™ or a simple notepad to write down the names of the people with whom you network. You will need some type of system to keep track of your contacts. Three-inch by five-inch index cards, spiral notebooks, personal organizers, or a computerized data base will work. Use a tracking system that is comfortable for you. Set up your network file to include the following contact information:

- Name of contact
- Address and telephone number
- How you met this person
- Occupation
- Date last contacted
- Conversation summary
- Names of referrals
- Date of thank-you letter
- Other comments

Maintaining Your Contacts

Keep in touch. Check in with your contacts every month to let them know how your job hunt is progressing. Keeping visible will generate further job leads. The key to faster success in your networking efforts is follow-up. The majority of follow-up calls aren't going to produce valuable new information or insights, but they'll succeed in reminding people of who you are. You will be gratified to see how often a follow-up call proves timely and serves to jog a contact's short-term memory.

You could also write a thank-you note to everyone you speak to. People like when others say thank-you, and your contacts may remember you a little better the next time you speak to them when you remember to thank them.

Job Leads

Employers frequently tell others when they are looking for job applicants. Through word of mouth, or what frequently is referred to as the "hidden job market," job-seekers and job-givers tie into each other through their networks.

Through networking, a trust factor is established. In other words, "if John referred you, then you must be okay." Coming to a prospective employer on the recommendation of a contact will give you a competitive edge over other candidates.

A 1989 study by the American Association of Counseling and Development (AACD) showed that:

* More than 50 percent of all jobs were found through networking, probably a conservative figure.
* Those jobs were frequently higher-paying, higher-status jobs.
* Twenty-five percent of those persons who got jobs through networking stayed longer.
* Better jobs were obtained through acquaintances than through friends.

Writing Your Inquiry Letter

The first impression you make on an Emergency Medical Service employer may be on paper. In all your written correspondence, you will want to make as good an impression as possible, so employers will be interested in giving you a personal interview. Your potential employer is likely to associate a letter that has a neat and clean appearance with good work habits and a sloppy one with bad work habits.

Also called a query letter or cover letter, this letter is written to the employer "inquiring" about the position opening, whether it be a specific opening or openings in general. A good cover letter should be neat, clear, brief, and most importantly, specific with no more than three or four paragraphs. You should send this letter to a specific person, either the personnel director or the department head for whom you would be directly working. If you don't know the person's name, call the EMS center and ask to whom you should write.

Begin your letter by explaining why you are writing. Let the person know that you are inquiring about possible job openings at the company, that you are responding to an advertisement in a particular publication, or that someone recommended that you write. Write your letter so it introduces the information on your resume, which you should include to call attention to your qualifications. Add information that shows you are suited for the job at whatever EMT level you are applying. Always thank readers for their attention to your letter, and add that you look forward to hearing from them soon.

Use the examples given to help create your own personalized cover letter.

Mary Van Doren
180 Meadow Court
City, State 12345
May 10, 1998

Mr. John Haroldson
St. Mary's Ambulance Center
P.O. Box 4545
City, State 12345

Dear Mr. Haroldson:

I am writing in query to your need for Emergency Medical Technicians within your ambulance center. I have heard many favorable things about your ambulance services, and I feel that this would be the perfect work environment for me. I am very interested in an available position.

I recently graduated from the EMT-Basic program at Med Tech Community College, and I received the required state and national certification. I have hands-on experience and training inside the Med Tech school's training ambulance center and believe I am in top physical condition, ready to begin work as an EMT-B.

I have always been interested in helping people, especially in emergency situations after having been traumatized myself. When I entered the EMT-Basic program, I realized my potential in becoming a great worker under pressure, as well as a caring individual for those under duress.

Enclosed is my resume, and I would be free to meet with you at your convenience. Also, I can arrange for you to speak with my references if you would like. Thank you for your attention to my letter. I can be reached at (343) 555-7676 or at the address above. I look forward to hearing from you.

Sincerely,

Mary Van Doren

Enc: Resume

Mike Anderson
1234 Darcey Ave.
Trellis, MD 12346
April 7, 1998

Ms. Joan Embers
Chark County Ambulance Service
P.O. Box 4456
City, State 12346

Dear Ms. Embers:

I am writing in response to your advertisement in the Sunday, March 23, 1998, *Maryland Journal and Constitution* newspaper. I have researched your emergency ambulance service and have found many attractive aspects that make your company an excellent work environment.

The advertisement stated that you are looking for someone with experience as an EMT-Intermediate. I am a recent graduate of North Maryland Technology's EMT-Intermediate Program, and I have the appropriate certification. I am looking for just this type of employment.

I have a good rapport with patients, doctors, and other EMTs, but most importantly, I am completely dedicated to my work. I knock myself out to make sure every victim rescued is treated with compassion and skill, and I don't need constant supervision or constant pats on the back to keep me working hard.

If you need an EMT-Intermediate who is good under pressure, experienced, and completely dedicated, I think we have something to talk about. I have the talent, the knowledge, and the training to be a successful EMT.

Enclosed is my resume, and I would be free to meet with you at your convenience. Thank you for your attention to my letter. I can be reached at (301) 555-1244 or at the address above. I look forward to hearing from you.

Sincerely,

Mike Anderson

Enc. [this is to specify that your resume is enclosed]

WRITING YOUR RESUME

The word *resume* originates from the French word *resumer*, meaning "to summarize," and that is exactly what you will do with your resume. Briefly outline your education, work experience, and special abilities and skills. This summary can act as your introduction by mail, as your calling card if applying in person, and as a convenient reference for yourself when filling out an application form or when being interviewed. In this field, a resume may or may not be required for getting a job.

The idea of a resume is to capture the interest of potential employers, so they will call you for a personal interview. That means you want to highlight the following sections:

- Objective
- Educational Background
- Work Experience
- Employment History
- Special Skills
- Related Experience
- Personal Qualifications

Select only those facts that point out your relevant skills and experiences. At the top of your resume, write your name, address, phone number, and e-mail address. Then, decide which items will be most interesting to the employer you plan to contact.

Objective

Under your name and address, you will need to state your job objective, which is your reason for contacting the employer. After the heading *Objective*, describe briefly the type of position for which you are applying, such as "To become an EMT-Basic."

Educational Background

Every interested employer will check your educational background, employment history, and may perform an in-depth background search. EMS, police, or fire employers do not want to hire someone who has a felony record or who has falsified their resume in any way. Make sure to use the correct and current name and address for each employer you've had and each school you've attended.

When listing this information, list your educational background first, beginning with the schools you have attended in reverse chronological order, starting with your most recent training and ending with the least recent. Employers want to know at a glance what your highest qualifications are. For each educational experience, include dates attended, name and location of school, and degree or certificate earned. It isn't necessary to include elementary school education.

Work Experience

List your related work experience. If you don't have any related work experience yet, find some way to connect summer jobs, volunteer work experience, or part-time jobs to your job objective. If you worked at a fast food restaurant for instance, depending upon your position, it may not be directly relevant; however, try to find some connection. If you were a manager at the restaurant, it would be appropriate to mention this job to show your managerial experience if you are applying for a managerial position. Or you could highlight your interaction with the customers since it is relevant to your future interaction with patients. If you've performed any volunteer work as an EMT, be sure to include it in this section. Clearly mark that the work was on a volunteer basis.

Special Skills

You may wish to include another section called "Special Skills," "Skills," or "Personal Qualifications." Write down any skills such as knowledge of medical language, knowledge of ambulance equipment, physical abilities, and any other related skill you posses that you think might help you land an EMT job.

Ways to Organize Your Resume

There are different ways you can organize your resume to highlight specific areas of experience. Some people may have work experience while others do not. The different styles allow you to organize your resume according to your skills and work history.

The Chronological Resume

You can present information about your employment history in different ways. The most common resume format is chronological—you summarize your work experience year by year.

Begin with your current or most recent employment and then work backward. For each job, list the name and location of the company for which you worked, the dates you were employed, and the position(s) you held. The order in which you present this information will depend on what you are trying to emphasize. If you want to call attention to the type or level of job you held, you should put the job title first. However, be consistent with whichever order you choose. Summer employment or part-time work should be labeled as such, and you will need to specify the months in the dates of employment for positions held less than a year.

The Functional Resume

The functional resume emphasizes what you can do rather than what you have done. It is useful for people who have large gaps in their work history or who have relevant skills that would not be properly highlighted in a chronological listing of jobs. The functional resume concentrates on your qualifications – anything from familiarity with hospital procedures to organizational skills or managerial experience. Specific jobs may be mentioned, but they are not the primary focus of this type of resume. This type of resume would be good for the person with little work experience.

The Combination Resume

You may decide that a combination of the chronological and functional resume would best highlight your skills. A combination resume allows for a mixture of your skill with a chronological list of jobs you've held. You get the best of both resumes. This is an excellent choice for students who have limited work experience and who want to highlight specific skills.

Sample Chronological Resume

JANICE LITTLE
1234 Murray Hill Drive • Dallas, TX 12345 • (214) 555-2143

OBJECTIVE

To obtain an EMT-Basic position.

EDUCATION

EMT-Basic certificate, June 1997
Med Tech Institute, 20 Troost Ave., Dallas, TX 12345
GPA: 3.95

Armadillo High School, Dallas, TX 12345, June, 1996
GPA: 3.98

WORK EXPERIENCE

Candy Striper, nurse aide volunteer, 1995-1996
St. Mary's Hospital, Dallas, TX 12345

- Served meals and helped patients eat, dress, and bathe
- Delivered messages and answered patient call bells
- Completed daily filing and answered telephones
- Inventoried, stored, and moved supplies

Assistant Evening Manager, 1994-1995
Texan Steer Restaurant, Dallas, TX 12345

- Began waiting on tables and greeting customers
- Took over arranging staff schedule
- Balanced register and deposited money
- Learned how to order food and soft drinks
- Managed personnel when manager was absent

AWARDS AND ACTIVITIES

Student of the Year, Med Tech Institute, Dallas, TX.

Volunteering at Oak View Nursing Home in Dallas, TX; swimming, running, kayaking, volunteering at local food shelters.

REFERENCES

References furnished upon request.

Sample Functional Resume

MIKE ANDERSON
1234 Darcey Ave.
Trellis, MD 12346
(301) 555-1244
e-mail: manders@server.com

OBJECTIVE: To obtain a position as an EMT-Intermediate.

VOLUNTEER EMT

- Two years volunteer experience as an EMT-Basic in volunteer fire station part-time
- Performed typical EMT-Basic duties
- Monitored patient status
- Kept ambulance in working condition

EMT-BASIC

- EMT-Basic for two years at private ambulance service
- Performed typical EMT-Basic duties
- Monitored patient status
- Kept ambulance in working condition

EDUCATION

- EMT-Intermediate certificate, March 1998.
  University of Maryland Medical Center, Trellis, Maryland.
  GPA: 3.8/4.0

- EMT-Basic certificate, January 1996.
  Medical Institute of Maryland, Trellis, MD.
  GPA: 3.9/4.0

REFERENCES

References furnished upon request.

Sample Combination Resume

Cathy Walters
1234 Glenwood Street • Glenwood, CO 12347 • (303) 555-4321

Objective:	To gain a career position as an EMT-Paramedic.
Qualifications:	Skilled EMT/Paramedic. Good rapport with patients. Expertise in all areas of Emergency Medical Services. Knowledgeable in life saving procedures. Devoted to patient care.
Education:	EMT-Paramedic certification, June 19xx. Colorado Mountain College, Glenwood Springs, CO. GPA: 3.8/4.0
	EMT-Intermediate certification, June 19xx. Colorado Mountain College, Glenwood Springs, CO. GPA: 4.0
	EMT-Basic certification, June 19xx. Colorado Mountain College, Glenwood Springs, CO. GPA: 3.8/4.0

Clinical Training: *Paramedic* training includes:
- Administering IV Therapy
- Advanced Cardiac Support
- Use of adjunctive equipment
- Drug administration

EMT-I and *EMT-B* training includes:
- CPR certification
- Patient care
- Cardiology
- Pharmacology
- Mega-codes
- Advanced airway management
- Ambulance up-keep

Related Experience: *EMT-Basic*, St. Francis Ambulance Center, Glenwood Springs, CO. 1/19xx-12/19xx.
- Performed typical EMT-Basic duties
- Monitored patient status
- Kept ambulance in working condition

EMT-Intermediate, Glenwood Springs County Fire Department. 2/19xx-12/19xx.
- Performed typical EMT-Intermediate duties
- Drove ambulance on occasion
- Performed advanced patient procedures
- Monitored patient status

References: References Available Upon Request

> **Resume Writing Tips**
>
> ♦ Be neat and organized.
>
> ♦ Increase your resume's legibility by effectively using white space.
>
> ♦ Try to limit resume to one page, but do not crowd. Go to two pages if necessary.
>
> ♦ Use action verbs.
>
> ♦ Be consistent in style.
>
> ♦ Be positive and confident in your resume, but don't lie or embellish.
>
> ♦ Don't be flashy or ostentatious – use white, cream, or gray paper.
>
> ♦ Go to your local library or bookstore to examine more sample resumes.

ACING YOUR INTERVIEW

The interview is the most important aspect of a job hunt because the impression you make on prospective employers could be the reason you do or don't get hired, or could determine where you become stationed and at what shift. The interview can also work in your favor to determine whether you would be compatible with the work environment. If you decide that you wouldn't want to work at that company during the interview, then it would be better to not accept the job offer.

EMT interviews are conducted much like any other interview. There will usually be more than one supervisor or personnel department head in the room with you. Many times this is so that they can combine as a group to discuss the potential of each candidate. Firefighter EMTs and Police officer EMTs often have oral interviews or oral boards, which take place in front of a fire or police chief and a panel of other personnel.

Some companies interview prospective EMTs twice if the supervisors who conduct your first interview think you are a good candidate. Interviewers are looking for specific qualities you may or may not have when asking questions, and the first impression you make is essential. Many people become nervous and have anxiety when attending an interview. To help you make it to the second interview or to the discussion of salary, here are some helpful tips to make your interviews go more smoothly.

Prepare for your Interview

Preparation will enable you to be confident, to overcome interviewing inexperience, and to sell yourself and your qualifications. You should bring your resume with you, even if the company already has it, and a personal inventory (a reference of possible answers to tough questions) for your own use. A personal inventory can guide you through describing your strengths and giving examples to support your resume. One way to create a personal inventory is to write a short personal autobiography. Having a small autobiography handy will help you remember the answers that may seem easier to remember when you don't feel "on the spot." This way you can remain confident throughout the interview.

Researching the EMS company you're applying to will make you feel more comfortable and will help prepare you to show genuine interest in the company during the interview. The public library and health publications are good sources for this kind of information. The idea is to converse knowledgeably about the EMS, police, or fire company during the interview.

Allow sufficient time for the interview. More than likely, you will be interviewing with more than one person during the interview cycle. You will not be at your best if you are worried about another appointment. It is a mistake to rush your interviewers because you have made a previous and conflicting commitment for the same day.

Arrive at the interview early. You would not want to arrive on the scene of an accident late. Arriving on time shows your respect for the interviewer and shows your professionalism. Allow extra travel time if you are unfamiliar with the employer's location to accommodate any delays.

Keep yourself in a positive frame of mind. Remember that you must be prepared to discuss job-related topics, not the interview's inconveniences or your personal problems. If your interview begins on a "down beat" it may be difficult to turn the atmosphere around into a positive situation later. Remember, turn the negative into a positive right away.

Plan to go to the interview alone. If your spouse or friend takes you to the interview, have him or her wait for you elsewhere. The presence of a third party can be a negative distraction for both you and the interviewer.

A hospital EMT supervisor and interviewer gives some advice about the interview procedure:

> The answers to the questions you are asked are the main points we
> look at when interviewing. If I ask you how you liked your past job,
> and you reply with how you hated it, that your boss was terrible, and
> the workers petty, then I know what kind of worker you will be. The

last thing you want to do is burn bridges with anyone who could be a reference. We want to see in you the traits that make a good EMT. Those qualities would be showing you are calm, that you can learn from mistakes, that you can make decisions quickly, and that you know how to treat patients.

Information Interview

Perform an *information interview* with an EMT professional you know who is already in the type of position you want. This will arm you with some knowledge of your interviewer's occupation and of your own interests, abilities, and values, so you will be better prepared on your job interview. Ask pertinent questions, get full information, take a tour of the facility, and you will be a step ahead of the competition. Here is a list of questions that will help you get the information you want in an information interview:

- Please give me a general description of the work you do.
- What is your typical work day like?
- What things do you find most rewarding about your work?
- What are the toughest problems or frustrations that you encounter in your job?
- What compromises are most difficult to make?
- If you could change your job in some way, what would that change be?
- What are the trade/professional/union groups to which you belong, and which do you find most beneficial in your work? Do any of them assist students who are interested in entry-level positions in your field?
- What abilities, interests, values, and personality characteristics are important for effectiveness and satisfaction in your field?
- How do people usually learn about job openings in your field?
- If you were hiring someone for an entry-level position in your field, what would be the critical factors influencing your choice of one candidate over another?
- Is there anything else you think I would benefit from knowing about this field?

Not only will you be more knowledgeable about your prospective position, but you will also gain interview experience, which may lessen the anxiety in your job interview.

Answering Tough Interview Questions

Employers tend to ask potential employees two kinds of questions: directive and open-ended. Directive questions attempt to gain, clarify, or verify factual information. Application forms are a series of directive questions. The open-ended question is an effort to draw out strengths and weaknesses. Watch out for illegal discriminatory questions. These questions probe for information that allows the listener to draw conclusions based on stereotypes or personal assumption about human behavior.

To deal effectively with all types of interview questions, you need to consider the employer's point of view, and remember to stay calm. No matter what kind of question is asked, an employer really has only three actual questions:

1. Can you do the work? (Do you have the skills, competence, credentials, etc.?)
2. Will you do the work? (Do you have the motivation and stamina to produce?)
3. Can you get along with others, especially with me, your supervisor? (What are your interpersonal skills and key personality traits?)

When responding to questions, ask yourself: what is the underlying question? This is particularly important with open-ended and illegally discriminatory questions. Accuracy and specificity are the keys to directive questions. The ability to understand yourself as a "product" and to express your strengths will help you answer open-ended questions more effectively.

Here are some interview questions that are frequently asked by employers:

• Why should we hire you?
• What are your career objectives?
• Tell me a little about yourself.
• If you could have the perfect position, what would it be?
• Do you have plans for continuing education?
• Why did you choose this career field?
• In what type of position are you most interested?
• What do you expect to be doing in five years?
• What is your previous work experience? What have you gained or learned from it?
• Why are you interested in our EMS company and in this particular opening?
• What do you consider to be your major strengths? Weaknesses?

- In what ways do you think you can make a contribution to our service?
- What two or three accomplishments have given you the most satisfaction?
- What have you done to show initiative and willingness to work?
- What journals do you subscribe to?
- What jobs have you enjoyed the most? The least? Why?
- What do you think determines an employee's progress in a good company?
- What qualifications do you have that make you feel you'll be successful in this field?

David Wesley, an EMT-Intermediate in San Diego, California, describes the EMT interviewing process:

> I wasn't very nervous during my interview. I knew I had the qualifications and initiative to do the job. Interviews today aren't as interrogative as they were ten years ago. In some of the older EMT or firefighters' day, the interview was more like an interrogation because employers could get away with it. Now, there are many questions that are illegal, so it really comes down to qualifications and personality.

Asking Questions

Frequently, toward the close of the interview, the interviewer will provide the opportunity to ask questions. Don't ever say that you don't have any questions. This is your chance to set yourself apart from the competition. Prepare your questions in advance. Ask the most important questions first in case there is not enough time to ask all of them. Do not ask questions which might show a lack of research. It is inappropriate to ask about salary and benefits unless the employer is offering you a position. Most employers do not want to discuss those issues until they are certain you are the right person for the job, so they will leave those issues for a second interview. Some examples of suitable questions are:

- Identify typical career paths based on past records. What is the realistic time frame for advancement?
- How is an employee evaluated and promoted? Is it company policy to promote from within? Is there a probationary period?
- Tell me about your initial and future training programs.
- What are the challenging facets of the job?
- What are the opportunities for personal growth?

- What are this company's plans for future growth?
- What is this EMS company's record of employment stability?
- What makes your emergency service different from your competitors?
- What are this EMS company's strengths and weaknesses?
- How would you describe your EMS company's personality and management style?

Follow-up Tactics

Send a courtesy letter to thank the interviewer for the opportunity to speak with her or him. Mention the time and date of the original interview and any important points discussed. Include important qualifications that you may have omitted in the interview, and reiterate your interest in the job.

Do not be discouraged if a definite offer is not made at the interview, or if a specific salary is not discussed. The interviewer will usually communicate with her or his office staff or interview other applicants before making an offer. Generally, a decision is reached within a few weeks. If you do not hear from an employer within the amount of time suggested during the interview, follow up with a telephone call. Show your commitment to their timetable. However, don't become a pest by calling every day for an answer.

Typical Hiring Procedures

Among most hospitals, private ambulance companies, and state or county run EMS facilities, the hiring procedures are about the same. These agencies normally require applicants to fill out an application for employment and participate in an interview. Depending on the area, you may or may not be able to fill out an application unless there is an opening. You can find out about openings through networking, job hot-lines, job boards, or human resources departments. Many employers prefer that you fill out the application on site, so remember to bring with you all necessary information you may not be able to readily recall. You should also bring along several copies of your resume, and turn in one with your application. Many times, an EMT supervisor, employment recruiter, or personnel department head will talk briefly with you at the time you turn in your application. Bringing everything with you will impress the employment recruiter.

For EMT positions, the employer will request that you take a drug test and a physical exam to ensure you are healthy and don't have a bad back. Also, employees normally conduct a criminal background check, a driving background check, and carefully screen your references. Each job description requires certain essential mental and physical capabilities as discussed in chapter one. The company supervisors assume you have the qualifications they are looking for because you completed the necessary training courses.

If you are planning to become a firefighter or police officer, you will have to endure physical tests such as ladder climbing or hose handling, training in a police academy or technical school, and you may be given additional mental scenario tests during an interview, or be required to meet with a psychiatrist or psychologist. Being honest, having good judgment, and a sense of responsibility are important because these public service positions are extremely important, so you will have to clear each of these hurdles before starting your new position.

The EMS facility may also offer a job description to you, so you may see the nature of the duties and experience required for the position for which you are applying. Job titles may differ in various institutions, but they are basically the same position. Here is an example of a job posting for an EMT-Basic from a hospital ambulance service:

Job Summary—EMT-Basic or EMT-A (Ambulance) or EMT-I (for level one)

Provides direct patient emergency care according to emergency policy and procedure. Contributes to the safe and effective operation of the ambulance unit. Provides life saving techniques for emergency patients.

Education	High school, EMT-Basic certification
Licensure	None
Experience	Previous exposure to training
Skills	Skills basic to completion of EMT-Basic course

Essential Physical and Mental Functions and Environmental Conditions

Able to communicate medically using medical terminology. Able to assess injury severity and perform CPR and other required basic life saving techniques.

Able to communicate calmly and rationally under pressure consistently.

Able to see objects far away frequently. Able to discriminate color and perceive depth frequently.

Able to give and receive verbal communications. Able to read and write written communications, such as reports.

Able to carry objects 10 pounds or more frequently; 49 pounds or less rarely.

Able to perform motor skills such as bending, twisting, turning, kneeling, reaching out, reaching up, wrist turning, grasping, finger manipulation, feeling perception, fast response, frequently.

Networking, searching classified advertisements, and keeping in touch with county, city, and state job hot-lines are the best methods for finding EMT positions. Job openings are posted at hospitals on average for about five days, and they can change weekly. Many hospitals also have a job hot-line number to keep up with job openings. Smaller EMS facilities may take out ads in the newspapers or consult local hospitals for applicants.

Application Process

The application process to become an EMT is straightforward. When there is an open position, you will fill out an application, and you will be required to perform a drug test and undergo a doctor's physical. Many hospitals will send you to a doctor through their employee health services. Your driving record will also be checked since nearly every EMT will be required to drive an ambulance at some time. Fire and police departments will be the only facilities to request a physical fitness test. Firefighters will be tested on their fitness level and ability to efficiently fight fires, and they will be required to have completed a firefighter training course. Police officer EMTs will also be tested on their fitness level, and they will be required to have completed a police officer training course.

Almost all county, state, and city hospital, fire, and police personnel offices do not take applications for EMTs or firefighters until positions become open. That could take months or years depending on the size of the community. Some smaller EMS companies take applications only once a year, but in larger, metropolitan cities where turnover is high and more ambulances are required to be ready, applications may be taken all year around. In the case of a smaller community, you may want to volunteer until a paid position opens.

If you have ever filled out an application for any kind of job, school, or financial aid before, the application for an EMT position will be similar. The main information the application will ask for is:

- name, address, and social security number
- job information or previous work experience, including dates and reason for leaving
- skills or supervisory experience
- educational experience
- criminal background information
- references, or you may be asked to sign a references release statement
- citizenship status

No question on the application form should touch upon a prospective employee's race, color, religion, national origin, age, sex, marital status, or disability. If there is a question on the application referring to any of these topics, you have the option of leaving it blank. The application should state that the company is an Equal Opportunity Employer.

You will be asked to sign the application to verify that all the information is true and correct. At the bottom, there may be a statement of understanding and reference release that states that any incorrect information is cause for immediate dismissal. Unfortunately, some people falsify information on their application. Remember that the employer will verify the information, so it's best to be honest. As an EMT supervisor of University Hospital in Jacksonville, Florida says:

> We have interviewed applicants that seem perfect for the position. Their answers to the questions we ask couldn't be more perfect, and their references look wonderful. That is until we check the references. One time it turned out that when we called a job reference, he told us not to hire the person. And, when we called the school listed, a representative said the person had never attended. My advice is never to falsify any information on your resume or application. Honesty is very important in your job as an EMT. We need to be able to trust you with people's lives. We were very disappointed but probably not as disappointed as the person who wasn't honest on the application.

Your application will stay active on file at a hospital for six months. If you have not called to update it, it will be kept in-active for another six months and then discarded. However, you may reapply or update your application at any time for other openings. In smaller EMS facilities, your application may or may not remain on file, depending on the size of the company. Smaller companies usually do not have as high of a turnover rate as hospitals, leaving little or no need to keep applications on file.

Driving an Ambulance

You'll be required to take an ambulance driving course before you will be hired as an EMT. The company may provide the training or you may be required to seek training on your own. The formal training program ensures that you can drive through various conditions, such as at high speed and on slick roads. Susan Carpenter, an EMT-B in Cary, North Carolina describes a driving test:

You also perform a road test once you've joined a company. One of the senior officers takes you out in an ambulance and gives you a street name. You need to be able to get him or her there the fastest, easiest way. This is called learning your district. They also teach you how to read road maps.

In many cases, in order to be hired as an EMT and get the ambulance training you need, you must have a clean driving record. Your driving record is as important as your passing the drug test. Many companies will not allow you to work for them if you do not have a clean driving record. Nearly every EMT will have to drive the ambulance at one point or another. That's what makes your driving record so important. In some private ambulance companies, you may ride as an assistant and not be allowed to drive.

The average EMS company regulations require you to have no more than two speeding tickets in the last three years and absolutely no DUIs (Driving Under the Influence). If you are already working and receive a DUI, you may be instantly terminated from the company.

Not only is having a clean driving record important, but your age is also important. Some hospitals and private EMS services require you to be of a certain age to be covered by insurance in case of an accident. That age range often starts from 21 to 25.

Sample Applications

See the sample applications on the following pages to get an idea of what you might be filling out as an initial step in becoming an EMT. These applications are provided as samples only, and they cannot be used to submit to any ambulance, fire, or police departments. You need to get an original application form from the appropriate department when you're ready to apply. However, you can read through these samples to find out what sort of information you'll be asked to provide, and to practice filling out the application. Don't underestimate this step. Filling out the application neatly and accurately can make or break your quest for employment because it's a key part of the employment process.

City of Sacramento
Employment Application
Department of Human Resources
921 10th Street, Room 101, Sacramento, CA 95814
Telephone: (916) 264-5726 / TDD: (916) 264-7388
An Equal Opportunity/Affirmative Action Employer

INSTRUCTIONS: *This application is part of the examination process. It must be completely filled out and signed to be accepted for review. Late and/or incomplete applications will be rejected.*

PLEASE PRINT OR TYPE
SOCIAL SECURITY NUMBER _____ - ____ - _____

JOB/EXAMINATION TITLE: _____

NAME _____
　　　　　Last　　　　　　　　　　First　　　　　　　　Middle Initial

MAILING ADDRESS: _____
　　　　　　Street #　　　　　　Street Name　　　　　　Apartment #

_____
City　　　　　　　　　State　　　　　　　　　Zip Code

Dept. of Human Resources Use Only	
App. Accepted	☐
App. Rejected	☐
Education	☐
Experience	☐
NMQ	☐
Late	☐
Other	☐

HOME PHONE ( )　　　　　　　OTHER PHONE ( )
ALL APPLICANTS, INCLUDING CITY EMPLOYEES, MUST IMMEDIATELY NOTIFY PERSONNEL SERVICES' STAFF, ROOM 200 AT THE ABOVE ADDRESS OF ANY ADDRESS OR PHONE CHANGES.

AGE: *If applying for a sworn position in law enforcement or the fire service, will you be 21 or older at the application deadline date?* _____ YES _____ NO

CALIFORNIA DRIVER LICENSE: *If required for position, do you have one?* ☐ Yes ☐ No
Dr. License # _____ Class _____ Expires _____

VETERAN'S PREFERENCE: Are you requesting Veteran's Preference? ☐ Yes ☐ No
To qualify for Veteran's Preference, a copy of Form DD214 must be submitted with this application. There are several criteria you must meet before qualifying for this preference. Please ask for the VETERAN'S PREFERENCE REGULATIONS sheet.

Active Duty - From _____ to _____

CONVICTIONS: Conviction of a crime is not necessarily a bar to employment. Each case is considered separately based on job requirements. However, failure to list convictions, except as provided below, may result in termination from the examination process or employment.
1. Have you ever been convicted by a court of a crime? ☐ Yes ☐ No
　Omit: a) Traffic violations (Driving Under the Influence Convictions must be reported).
　Omit: b) Any conviction committed prior to your 18th birthday which was finally adjudicated in Juvenile Court or under a youth offender law.
　Omit: c) Any incident sealed under Welfare and Institutions Code S781 or Penal Code S1203.45.

2. If "YES" state WHAT conviction, WHEN, WHERE, AND DISPOSITION OF CASE. _____

CITY EMPLOYMENT:
1. Are you currently employed by the City of Sacramento? ☐ Yes ☐ No
　If "YES", what department? _____
2. If "NO", have you ever been employed by the City of Sacramento? ☐ Yes ☐ No
　If "YES", what department? _____
　If you were previously employed by the City of Sacramento under another name, please state other name(s). _____
3. Please check the type(s) of work you will accept:
　☐ Permanent employment　☐ Full-time　☐ Part-time　☐ Temporary (12 months maximum in any one job).

EDUCATION AND TRAINING:
Complete this section if required for job. Submit verification of your education such as copies of transcripts or diplomas.
High School Graduate or Passed GED? ☐ Yes ☐ No

NAME AND LOCATION OF COLLEGE, UNIVERSITY, BUSINESS, CORRESPONDENCE, TRADE OR SERVICE SCHOOL(S)	MAJOR COURSE OF STUDY	Completed # of		Diploma, Certificate, or Degree Received, # Hours of Training Program, or Course(s) Required by Job Announcement
		Semester Units	Quarter Units	

Current certificates of professional competence, licenses, membership in professional associations.

_____
_____

EMPLOYMENT QUESTIONNAIRE

APPLICANT: Please complete both sides of this section and submit it with your application. This completed section is confidential and will be detached from your application. This information is voluntary and is gathered in accordance with State and Federal laws for the purpose of evaluating the effectiveness of our Affirmative Action and recruitment efforts.

CHECK MALE OR FEMALE.　☐ Male ☐ Female
ALSO, PLEASE CHECK ONE BOX ONLY FOR THE RACIAL/ETHNIC CATEGORY YOU MOST CLOSELY IDENTIFY WITH.
(SEE BELOW FOR THE ETHNIC DEFINITIONS.)

☐ White — (Not Hispanic origin) All persons having origins in any of the original peoples of Europe, North Africa, or the Middle East.
☐ Black — (Not of Hispanic origin) All persons having origins in any of the Black racial groups of Africa.
☐ Hispanic — All persons of Mexican, Puerto Rican, Cuban, any other Spanish Hispanic (does not include persons of Portuguese or Brazilian origin or persons who acquire Spanish surname).
☐ Asian or Pacific Islander — All persons having origins in any of the original peoples of the Far East, Southeast Asia, the Indian Subcontinent, or the Pacific Islands (excluding the Philippine Islands). This area includes, for example, China, Japan, Korea, and Samoa.
☐ American Indian or Alaskan Native — All persons having origins in any of the original peoples of North America, and who maintain cultural identifications through tribal affiliation or community recognition. Please identify your tribal affiliation: _____

☐ Filipino — All persons having origins in the Philippine Islands.

- REVERSE SIDE MUST BE COMPLETED -

JOB/EXAMINATION TITLE: _____ NAME_____
                                                         Last   First   Middle Initial

QUALIFYING EXPERIENCE: *List experience which relates to the qualifications required on the Job Announcement. Begin with your most recent experience. List all jobs separately. The experience you list will be used to determine if you meet the qualifications stated on the job announcement. Applications that do not list related experience will be considered incomplete and will be rejected. A resume will not substitute for the information required in this section. Your application will be rejected if you write "See Resume".*

NOTE: If you have additional experience and/or comments, please attached another sheet. Qualifying experience is based on 40 hours per week (pro-rated if less than 40 hours/week).

FROM: MO. DAY YR.	TITLE:	PRESENT OR MOST RECENT EMPLOYER:
TO: MO. DAY YR.	DUTIES:	
Total time: YR. MO.		ADDRESS:
HOURS per WEEK:		
# PEOPLE SUPERVISED:		PHONE:
MONTHLY SALARY:		SUPERVISOR:
		May we contact? ☐ YES ☐ NO

FROM: MO. DAY YR.	TITLE:	FORMER EMPLOYER:
TO: MO. DAY YR.	DUTIES:	
Total Time: YR. MO.		ADDRESS:
HOURS per WEEK:		
# PEOPLE SUPERVISED:		PHONE:
MONTHLY SALARY:		SUPERVISOR:
		May we contact? ☐ YES ☐ NO

FROM: MO. DAY YR.	TITLE:	FORMER EMPLOYER:
TO: MO. DAY YR.	DUTIES:	
Total Time: YR. MO.		ADDRESS:
HOURS per WEEK:		
# PEOPLE SUPERVISED:		PHONE:
MONTHLY SALARY:		SUPERVISOR:
		May we contact? ☐ YES ☐ NO

FROM: MO. DAY YR.	TITLE:	FORMER EMPLOYER:
TO: MO. DAY YR.	DUTIES:	
Total Time: YR. MO.		ADDRESS:
HOURS per WEEK:		
# PEOPLE SUPERVISED:		PHONE:
MONTHLY SALARY:		SUPERVISOR:
		May we contact? ☐ YES ☐ NO

I CERTIFY that all statements in this application are true and complete. I agree and understand that any misstatements or omissions of material facts herein will cause forfeiture on my part of all rights to employment with the City of Sacramento. I understand that if I do not meet the announced requirements, I will be eliminated from the examination process, and that applications must be received by the City Department of Human Resources at 921 10th Street, Room 101, Sacramento CA 95814, by 5:00 p.m. on the final filing date specified on the Job Announcement. **POSTMARKS ARE NOT ACCEPTED.** I herby authorize the city to verify the accuracy of the information I have provided on this application.

SIGNATURE: _____   DATE:_____
           (Required for application to be complete)

THIS APPLICATION AND ALL ATTACHMENTS ARE CONSIDERED PROPERTY OF THE CITY OF SACRAMENTO DEPARTMENT OF HUMAN RESOURCES. PHOTOCOPIES WILL <u>NOT</u> BE FURNISHED. PLEASE ATTACH <u>COPIES</u> OF YOUR ORIGINAL DOCUMENTS.

Job/Examination Title: _____
I first learned of this job opening through (check one only):

☐ A Friend or Relative
☐ The City's Department of Human Resources Job Line or Walk In
☐ Contact with a City Department/Employee
   If Department, Specify Which _____
☐ An Organization or Group (Specify) _____
☐ An Advertisement (Specify Newspaper, Publication,
   TV or Radio Station) _____
☐ Other Means (Specify) _____

Do you have any physical or mental impairment which may limit your ability to perform the job applied for?   ☐ YES   ☐ NO
If yes, what can be done to accommodate your limitations and, if necessary, to provide assistance in the testing process?

_____

_____

Revised January 25, 1996/FRM2-16.C

PER 029

CITY OF HOUSTON
PERSONNEL DEPARTMENT
P.O. BOX 1562
HOUSTON, TEXAS 77251

**EMPLOYMENT
APPLICATION**

An Equal Opportunity Employer

Please Print In Ink Or Type

Position:	PN#	Today's Date

PERSONAL

Last Name	First	Middle	Social Security # Must be verified

No.	Street	City	State	Zip	Home Phone	Business/Alternate Phone

U. S. Citizenship ☐ YES NO ☐

If not a citizen, do you possess a work authorization?

Number and Type

If you have ever been convicted of an offense (excluding minor traffic violations) complete the following:

Charge	Place of Arrest	Date	What Disposition was Made?

Please list below any relatives, including those by marriage, employed by the City:

Name of Relative	Relationship	Department	Position

Have you ever been employed by the City of Houston? ☐ YES NO ☐

	Position Held	Date of Separation

Under what name did you appear on payroll?

EDUCATION

Name & Location	Date Graduated		Degree	If no, highest yr or hrs compl.	Major
	YES	NO			
High School					
College or University					
Graduate School					
Trade/Business/Technical					
Armed Service School					

MILITARY

Branch of Service	Service Dates		Rank at Discharge	Are you now a member of any military or naval organization?
	From	To		☐ YES NO ☐

Do you have a valid Texas driver's license? ☐ YES NO ☐

(TEXAS DRIVER'S LICENSE NUMBER)
(Class A, P, or C)

PER 029 REV. 2/93

Do Not Write In This Space

List below beginning with your most recent, all present and past employment.
Please complete in full.

	Name & Address of Company	Position, Dates Emp. & Salary		Supv. Name & Title	Reason for Leaving
1			Name	
		From Mo/Yr	Current $		
		To Mo/Yr	Final $	Title	
2				Name	
		From Mo/Yr			
		To Mo/Yr	Final $	Title	
3				Name	
		From Mo/Yr			
		To Mo/Yr	Final $	Title	
4				Name	
		From Mo/Yr			
		To Mo/Yr	Final $	Title	
5				Name	
		From Mo/Yr			
		To Mo/Yr	Final $	Title	

EMPLOYMENT HISTORY

List below three references (other than relatives)

Name	Phone	Address	Employer

REFERENCES

MAY WE CONTACT YOUR PRESENT EMPLOYER FOR REFERENCE? _____

PLEASE READ CAREFULLY BEFORE SIGNING: I certify that all the information provided by me in connection with my application, whether on this document or not, is true and complete, and I understand that any misstatement, falsification, or omission of information shall be grounds for refusal to hire or, if hired, termination. I authorize any of the persons, organizations, and educational institutions referenced in this application to give officials of the City of Houston any and all information concerning my previous employment, education, or any other information they might have, personal or otherwise, with regard to any of the subjects covered by this application, and I release all such parties from all liability from any damages which may result from furnishing such information to the City of Houston.

I UNDERSTAND THAT ALL PERSONS OFFERED EMPLOYMENT BY THE CITY OF HOUSTON MUST SUCCESS-FULLY PASS A DRUG TEST AS A CONDITION OF EMPLOYMENT.

_____
Signature of Applicant

_____
Date

THE INSIDE TRACK

Who:	Susan Carpenter
What:	Volunteer EMT-Basic
Where:	Cary EMS
	Cary, North Carolina
How long:	Since February 1997
Degree:	EMT-B Certification; working on Nursing Degree

Insider's Advice

I originally wanted to be a nurse, but circumstances prevented me from finishing my associate degree. Until I can go back to nursing school, I decided to take the classes to become an EMT-Basic. Basically, I wanted to help people. I have a blast doing it. Every time the buzzer and the pagers go off, I get butterflies in my stomach. You get accustomed to it but never used to it. If I gave any advice to someone wanting to become an EMT, it would be to find a squad in your area, and ask if you can ride with them a couple of times as an observer to see if you like it. Most places do not mind, but they do ask that you have some preliminary vaccinations first, such as tuberculosis, hepatitis, etc. When you ride along like this, you get a chance to see firsthand what being an EMT is really like and if you could handle the job.

Insider's Take on the Future

I plan on getting my Automated External Defibrillator certification to allow for more experiences as an EMT. Then, I plan on going back to nursing school to complete my associate degree and become a registered nurse. Although I enjoy my work as an EMT—you can't be in this work if you don't—and may miss the fast pace of going on calls, I want more time with patients to care for them and get to know them.

CHAPTER | 3

This chapter discusses training programs: how to evaluate them and how to choose the right one for you. You'll find out about entrance requirements and you'll be given some key questions to ask about the training program you're interested in. You will also find sample course descriptions, as well as an extensive directory of schools that offer EMT-Basic, EMT-Intermediate, and EMT-Paramedic courses.

EMT TRAINING PROGRAMS

All jobs in the EMS field require some period of training in a clinical setting, involving direct patient treatment and operating equipment, in order for you to gain knowledge of necessary life-saving procedures. Requirements for entering the EMT field include completing a training program and obtaining the appropriate certificate.

MAKING DECISIONS ABOUT TRAINING

Deciding on the right training program for you may seem challenging if your interest in becoming an EMT is combined with firefighting, police, or rescue work. Remember the personal evaluation you created in chapter one? Use that evaluation to consider the questions below. Though you may not know the answers right away, this checklist of questions can help you to choose a training program that is right for you and to tailor your career goals to a specific EMT position. Answer the questions as best as you can now, or come back to them later.

- Do I need a job now or can I wait and gain greater experience through education?
- How long do I want to be in school before getting a job as an EMT?
- What schools are in my area?
- Can I or do I want to relocate?
- Can I visit the school?

You will need to know if you can afford to relocate. Many times, schools and jobs are not available in your community but they are in your state. Can you afford moving expenses? Can you afford to rent an apartment? If you want to attend an out-of-state school, you should expect your tuition to nearly double. Always visit the school of your choice to find out if it will meet your needs before you apply.

- What kind of certification or degree do I want to complete?
- In what kind of facility do I want to work?
- What is the salary level I'd like to have?
- Who are the kinds of coworkers I'd like to have?

These questions may be the most important to ask yourself. They will determine what kind of job you will actually train for. You should research career options by visiting hospital ambulance services, fire stations, police departments, private ambulance services, and other health organizations in your area to find out what type of work environment they have and what the workers there are like. Also, research the salary options of the job you want from the health centers in your area because the salary descriptions in chapter one are general and not region-specific.

While it's important to set goals for your career, be open to trying or researching work environments that you might not have originally considered. There's also no need to lock yourself into something permanent after school. You may instead decide to further your education in order to move up in status and salary.

As discussed in chapter one, certification is required for all EMT careers. When you sign up for a particular training program, you will be informed as to the requirements of the course. After you have graduated, you will take the state or national certification examinations before going on to employment.

TYPES OF TRAINING PROGRAMS

The educational requirements for the different EMT occupations generally range from one- to two-year (or longer) certificate programs to two-year associate degrees. Training for entry-level positions is offered in community colleges, technical schools, colleges, universities, and the armed forces, depending upon the type of program you are seeking. Programs provide both classroom and clinical instruction.

High School Preparation

If you haven't yet completed high school, you can take courses that will help you to prepare for becoming an EMT while you are still in school. First of all, make sure that you have a handle on basic skills such as reading comprehension, writing, computer literacy, and basic mathematics and science. To go even further with your training, take as many of the following classes as possible:

Health
Science
Driver Education or Defensive Driving
English
Physical Education (P.E.)
Computer Training
Spanish or other language

By building a strong educational foundation while still in high school, you'll increase your chances of succeeding in the next phase of your training, whether it's a certificate, an associate degree, or an on-the-job training program.

EMT Training Program Entrance Requirements

To be admitted into a basic EMT training program, applicants must be at least eighteen years old, have a high school diploma or GED, and have a valid driver's license. Exact requirements of the various levels of the EMT courses vary slightly in different states. Placement exams may be required for first-time students, and in some training courses, those under 18 may have to sign a waiver to attend the program. Many EMTs first become interested in the field while in the U. S. Armed Forces, where they may have received training as medics, whereas others become EMTs after having their lives saved by one.

Another entrance requirement is to have the right attitude. Jeanine L. Hoffman, an EMT-Basic Instructor from Landisville, Pennsylvania says:

What I look for in students and what they must possess are two different items. What they MUST have is a willingness to learn, ability to arrive on time to every class, and the ability to change their way of thinking. Many people think of EMS as how they see it on "COPS" or "Rescue 911." Once they get into class they need to change those misconceptions and realize that we don't save everyone, and some people try to hurt us when we try to help them. As to what I would like to see every student enter class with—again a willingness to learn, a wish to help others, a respect for other people, and a mature attitude toward their studies. Things like a background in medicine or fire service are nice but not needed. We can teach the skills, but the attitude is something the students need to possess.

Depending on which school or college they attend, many incoming students need to complete entrance exams, such as the Science Placement Test (SPT) or the College Placement Test (CPT), which are tests that determine a student's placement in courses. These tests evaluate reading, writing, and math skills, so if you score low in math and high in science, you may be placed in a remedial math course such as Math 099 to use as review before taking Math 101.

Other criteria used in admitting applicants to programs may include the College Board SAT exam, which you may have taken already in high school; the American College Test; high school grade point average; recommendation letters; and personal statements.

Some schools also require students to take a physical and have blood work done to check for any diseases that may be contagious. Students may also have to purchase health insurance if they are not already covered by their parents or by their personal coverage. The school should offer a liability or malpractice insurance policy at a small fee to its students and explain the coverage.

EMT-Basic Training Program

Formal training is needed to become an EMT-Basic. EMT-Basic training is 100 to 120 hours of classroom work, plus 10 hours of internship in a hospital emergency room. Training is offered by police, fire, health departments, hospitals, and colleges.

Here is an example of a 23 credit, two semester EMT-Basic course from a community college in Annandale, Virginia for a one-year Occupational Emergency Technician Basic Certificate.

First Semester

Basic Emergency Medical Technician/Ambulance

Prepares students for certification as a Virginia and National Registry EMT/A. Includes all aspects of pre-hospital basic life support as defined by the Department of Transportation's National Curriculum for Basic EMTs/Ambulance. Lecture—4 hours. Class meets 8 hours a week. 6 credit hours.

Coordinated Practice

Supervised practice in selected health agencies coordinated by the College. Credit/practice ratio maximum 1:5 hours. Variable hours. 1 credit hour.

College Composition

Prerequisites are a satisfactory score on appropriate English proficiency exams and four units of high school English or equivalent. Develops writing ability for study, work, and other areas of writing based on experience, observation, research, and reading of selected literature. Lecture—3 hours a week. 3 credit hours.

Human Biology

Surveys the structure and function of the human body. Applies principally to students who are not majoring in science fields. Lecture—4 hours a week. 4 credit hours.

Second Semester

Principles of Extrication

Prerequisite is EMT/A certification. Focuses on the practical evolution utilized for vehicle extrication, basic and light duty rescue. Includes techniques of vehicle, water, vertical, and trench rescue, as well as electrical emergencies, bus, aircraft, and subway crashes, radiation hazards, and elevator accidents. Lecture—2 hours a week. Lab—4 hours a week. Class is 6 hours a week. 4 credit hours.

EMT Elective

Two credit hours.

Introduction to Medical Terminology

Focuses on medical terminology for students preparing for careers in the health profession. Lecture—2 hours a week. 2 credit hours.

General Elective

Computer Operating Elective. 1 credit hour.

The in-state tuition at this community college is $48.00 per credit hour and the out-of-sate tuition is $157.35 per credit hour.

EMT-Intermediate Training Program

EMT-Intermediate training generally includes 35-55 hours of additional instruction after the EMT-Basic training is completed. Exact requirements needed to become an EMT-Intermediate vary from state to state. Here is an example of a 24-26 credit hour EMT-Intermediate training program from a community college in Tucson, Arizona.

Intermediate Emergency Medical Technology I

Prerequisite EMT 151 (EMT-Basic completion). Continuation of training in techniques of pre-hospital emergency medical care and examination of aspects of human anatomy and physiology surveyed in EMT 151. Includes pharmacology; the respiratory, cardiovascular, and central nervous systems; soft tissue and musculoskeletal injuries; obstetrics/gynecological emergencies; rescue techniques; and communications. 6 credit hours. 7 periods; 6 lecture and 1 lab.

Intermediate Emergency Medical Technology II

Continuation of training in techniques of pre-hospital emergency medical care. The recognition, management, and pathophysicology involved with the respiratory, nervous, and cardiovascular systems. Expands on disorders of hydration, including progression of shock. Also includes a study of blood and its components and techniques of management. Emphasis on patient assessment and the importance of report writing. 4 credit hours. 5 periods; 4 lecture and 1 lab.

Intermediate Emergency Medical Technology III

Continuation of training in techniques of pre-hospital emergency medical care. Includes method used by the I-EMT for interviewing in a medical emergency and for handling medical emergencies with exposure to environmental extremes. 4 credit hours. 5 periods; 4 lecture and 1 lab.

Intermediate Emergency Medical Technology IV

Continuation of training in techniques of pre-hospital emergency medical care. Includes techniques involved in rescue, communications, and the systems approach to medical emergencies with emphasis on oral evaluation and skills evaluation. Also provides rotations through clinical settings, which allows for further exposure to I-EMT skills. 4 credit hours. 5 periods; 4 lecture and 1 lab.

Writing Fundamentals

Review of sentence structure, mechanics, and usage. Includes paragraph development and short essay organization. 3 credit hours. 3 periods.

Science or Math Elective

Three credit hours.

Communications

Three credit hours.

In-state tuition for this community college in Arizona is $32.00 per credit hour, and out-of-state is $55.00 per credit hour with a $15.00 application fee.

EMT-Paramedic Training Program

Training programs for EMT-Paramedics generally include between 750 and 2,000 hours, and you can enroll in a certificate or associate degree program. Here is an example of a two-year associate degree program for the EMT-Paramedic from a community college in Arnold, Maryland.

Introduction to Paramedic Practice

Prerequisite(s) EMT-Intermediate course completion, a score of 19 or better on the Allied Health Arithmetic Placement Test, and permission of the EMT department head. Introduces the paramedic student to advanced life support concepts and interventions. Emphasizes infection control, basic and advanced airway management, patient assessment techniques, and principles of pharmacology. Students are expected to practice selected procedures on each other during college lab. Lab fee $40. 5 credit hours.

Shock and Trauma

Overview of kinematics of trauma, victim rescue theory, and skills and pathophysiology of shock. Includes the study of body fluids, electrolytes, and management of electrolyte imbalances. Rescue skills practice coordinated with Anne

Arundel County Fire Department Training Division. Students practice selected procedures on each other during college lab. Lab fee $40. 4 credit hours.

ECG Interpretation

Presents cardiac wave form interpretations including cardiac anatomy, physiology, and electrical conduction. Addresses total cardiac arrest performance sequence, use of automatic and manual cardiac defibrillator, and state protocols. ECG recognition practiced in college lab. You are expected to practice selected procedures on each other during college lab. Lab fee $20. 3 credit hours.

ALS Unit Practicum

Introduces the role of the advanced life support provider in the field. Students perform selected advanced life support skills in the pre-hospital environment under the direction of paramedic preceptors. 2 credit hours. 10-hour clinical practicum weekly.

Medical and Trauma Emergencies

Comprehensive study of disease entities and trauma. Emphasizes pharmacologic intervention and advanced management of emergency conditions. Covers cardiovascular, respiratory, nervous system, abdominal cavity, endocrine, and environmental emergencies as a physiologic base for assessment and pre-hospital intervention. Students are expected to practice selected procedures on each other during college lab. Lab fee $25. 10 credit hours. 116 hours of lecture, 30 hours of college laboratory, 73 hours of clinical practicum; one semester.

Special Patients

Emphasizes the unique emergencies and pre-hospital management of special population groups. Includes maternal and newborn care, pediatric emergencies, geriatric patient management, chemical dependence, and behavioral emergencies. Students' experience will be gained in college lab and clinical lab. Lab fee $25. 5 credit hours.

Advanced Paramedic Practicum

Practice comprehensive patient assessment and intervention in specialty facilities and on advanced life support units under direct supervision. Includes a final written preparatory review exam, advanced practical skills review, and mock practical exam. Lab fee $25. 3 credit hours.

Special Topics: Emergency Medical Technology

Permits qualified cardiac rescue technicians and EMT-Paramedic students to meet updated certification and competency requirements or to complete necessary course-work to be eligible to take the state CRT exam or the state EMT-Paramedic exam. Lab fee $0-50. 1-4 credit hours.

In-state tuition at this community college in Maryland is an average of $1,740 per year, and out-of-state tuition is an average of $6,060 per year.

CHOOSING THE TRAINING PROGRAM THAT'S RIGHT FOR YOU

You should find out all you can about the school(s) you want to attend. Finding out the details will save time, money, and energy in the long run. Talk to former students and people who are currently in the program to evaluate the curriculum offered at each school. If there is a choice of schools in your area, pick the one that will fit your life and study habits as much as possible.

Contact the schools that are in your community to find out more information about the programs they offer. You can find out what schools offer EMT-related courses by looking in the directory listed in the second half of this chapter. You should confirm that each school you are considering is currently offering courses that are related to emergency medical services. Ask to speak to a guidance counselor or to someone in the emergency medical services department to get detailed information about the EMT programs that are offered by each school. Request a school catalog and whatever brochures are available about the school and its programs. Read these documents carefully when you receive them, especially the fine print in the college catalog. You want to find out exactly what courses are required for your program, how much the program will cost, and how long the program will last.

Another thing you can do, if you have the time, is to visit the schools in your area and talk to a guidance counselor in person at each one. These counselors are trained to help you identify your needs and decide if their school will meet those needs. Follow these steps when preparing for an on-campus visit:

- Contact the office of admissions to request an appointment to visit. Remember to ask for the name of the person making the appointment and the person you will be meeting with. Try to schedule a meeting with an instructor in the EMT program as well as a guidance counselor in the admissions or counseling department.

- Bring a copy of your high school transcript or permanent record card if you will have the opportunity to meet with an admissions counselor during your visit.

- Include a list of honors or awards you have received in high school or the community, including documentation of any EMT volunteer experience or other medical training.

- Ask to tour the EMT laboratories or practical experience areas, if available. This tour should show you the available equipment and materials for emergency simulations and other EMT exercises. Many schools are affiliated with one or more local hospitals, fire departments, or ambulance services, so they offer this hands-on training through another agency.

Be prepared to ask questions about the school and surrounding community, including extracurricular activities, work opportunities, and anything else you don't find explained in the promotional brochures.

Asking the Right Questions

After you visit several schools and narrow your choices down to two or three schools, the next step is to ask tough questions about each program to make the final selection. Here are some important questions you should ask about a prospective school to see if it measures up to your standards. After each question, you'll find sample answers that you should receive or other considerations that you should think about before choosing a particular school.

What requirements will I need to attend?

Check with each school you are considering to find out what its specific entrance requirements are. Requirements vary from school to school. For instance, you may be required to do any one or more of the following:

- Take English, math, or science placement tests
- Take and achieve a certain score on the SAT or ACT if you have not already taken them in high school
- Have a certain level GPA from high school
- Take a physical exam

If you feel that you won't have any trouble meeting the entrance requirements for your targeted schools, then you're all set. If one of the schools you are considering has an entrance requirement that you think you may not meet, call an admissions counselor and discuss your particular case with her or him. Most schools will at least offer some type of remedial help if needed, so students can meet the requirement in the future.

Is the program I chose accredited? By whom?

It is very important that your school be accredited to know you are getting the best education possible that meets high standards. There are many agencies that accredit programs in every field of the healthcare industry. See Appendix A for a list of accrediting agencies. Be sure your targeted school lists one or more of them as their accrediting agency. An important point to remember is that if the school you choose is not accredited, you cannot get financial aid through any of the government programs. (See chapter four for more information about how to obtain financial aid.)

How much does the program cost?

You need to determine what school you can afford to attend. Find out how much tuition and application fees will cost at each school you are considering. Also ask financial aid administrators what kind of financial aid is available from the school. Can you receive enough financial aid to attend a large college or university? How much are tuition, books, and tools going to cost?

The amount of money you have and the amount the training program is going to cost may determine whether you should work part time and go to school part time, apply for financial aid, and whether you can afford a technical institute or a college.

What are the faculty members' qualifications and how experienced are they?

There should be some faculty members who have advanced degrees, such as EMT-Paramedic, and who have many years of experience in the working world. The faculty should be accessible for student conferences.

What is the student/teacher ratio?

The student-teacher ratio is a statistic that shows the average number of students assigned to one teacher in a classroom or lab. It's important that the student-teacher ratio not be too high. Education suffers if classrooms are too crowded, or if a teacher has too many students to be able to see everyone who wishes to be seen for a private conference.

According to one of the top national accrediting agencies—the Accrediting Council for Independent Colleges and Schools—a reasonable student-teacher ratio for skills training is 30 students to 1 teacher in a lecture setting and 15 students to 1 teacher in a laboratory or clinical instruction setting. At very good schools the ratio is even better than what the ACICS recommends.

What percentage of graduates of the EMT program were placed in jobs upon graduation?

The placement rate for graduates can be important, and when considering a school, whether small or large, you should ask what it is. Many schools offer free placement services for the working lifetime of their graduates.

Is the school equipped with the latest EMT equipment and ambulance technology?

When you visit the school you plan to attend, ask to see their laboratory facilities and ambulance technology and equipment. The most recent and advanced computer technology and training equipment should be available to students. Some examples of the type of equipment you should look for are Automated External Defibrillators, heart monitors, and intravenous (I.V.) supplies.

When are classes scheduled?

Find out if the school you're considering offers any weekend or evening classes. If you need to work full time during regular business hours while attending school, you'll need to find a school that offers classes at non-traditional times.

Is the campus environment suitable?

When you visit the school, determine how the campus feels to you. Is it too big? Too small? Too quiet? Is the campus in a bustling city or rural community? Is it easily accessible? Do you need to rely on public transportation to get there? Select a school that has a campus environment that meets your needs.

Does the school offer child care facilities?

This may or may not be of concern to you. If it is, you'll want to tour the child care facilities and interview the people who work in the child care center to see if the care is suitable for your children.

Application Tips from Admissions Directors

♦ Apply as early as you can. You'll need to fill out an application and submit high school or GED transcripts and any copies of SAT, ACT, or other test scores used for admission. If you haven't taken these tests, you may have to before you can be admitted. Call the school and find out when the next program starts, then apply at least a month or two prior to make sure you can complete requirements before the program begins.

♦ You may receive a pre-written request for high school transcripts from the admissions office when you get your application. Make sure you send those requests as soon as possible, so the admissions process is not held up in any way.

♦ Make an appointment as soon as possible to take any placement tests that may be required.

♦ Pay your fees before the deadline. Enrollment is not complete each quarter or semester until students have paid all fees by the date specified on their registration form. If fees are not paid by the deadline, their classes may be canceled. If you are going to receive financial aid, apply as early as you can.

♦ Find out if you must pass a physical or have any other medical history forms on file for the school you choose early in the application process, so this does not hold up your admission.

MAKING THE MOST OF YOUR TRAINING PROGRAM

After you accept the responsibility of entering a training program to receive a certificate or degree, you want to make the most of your training experience. If your county or EMS company is paying for your training, you will probably have to repay them if you drop out. It is important to take your classes seriously, study hard, and take advantage of the opportunities your school offers to get your money's worth and to have the opportunity to apply for any job you want. EMT instructor Jeanine Hoffman shares the advice she gives most often to students:

> I tell them to RELAX! You don't have to go out on the street your first day and handle a situation like the World Trade Center Bombing. It's a gradual learning process and everything will fit into the schedule and build upon everything that came before it. Knowing this sometimes helps students to alleviate their fears because students tend to fear panic at certain times during the EMT course. If they read ahead, keep up with their studies, pay attention in class, and use their practical and free time wisely, they will do just fine.

DIRECTORY OF EMT TRAINING PROGRAMS

Now that you've decided to get into a training program, you need to find one at a school near you. In the rest of this chapter, you will find a directory of schools that offer EMT training programs listed by state and alphabetized within each state by city. There are hundreds of vocational, technical, military, and university institutions that offer EMT-Basic and Intermediate certificates and Paramedic associates degrees in cities across the country.

All programs provide school name, address, and phone number, so you can contact each school directly to get more information and application forms for the programs that interest you. This listing is intended to help you begin your search for an appropriate school. The specific schools included in this listing, however, are not endorsed or recommended by LearningExpress. Always contact the schools you are considering to get current information on program requirements and areas of specialization before you apply.

ALABAMA
Lurleen B. Wallace State Junior College
P.O. Box 1418, Hwy 84 East
Andalusia 36420-1418
334-222-6591

James H. Faulkner State Junior College
Hammond Circle
Bay Minette 36507
205-580-2100

Bessemer State Technical College
P.O. Box 308
Bessemer 35021
205-428-6391

Jefferson State Community College
2601 Carson Road
Birmingham 35215
205-853-1200

University of Alabama at Birmingham
UAB MJH 107 2010
Birmingham 35294-2010
205-934-4011

John C. Calhoun State Community
College
P.O. Box 2216
Decatur 35609-2216
205-306-2500

George C. Wallace State Community
College-Dothan
Route 6, Box 62
Dothan 36303-9234
334-983-3521

Gadsen State Community College
1001 George Wallace Drive
Gadsen 35902-0227
205-549-8210

Wallace State Community College-
Hanceville
801 Main Street Northwest
P.O. Box 2000
Hanceville 35077-2000
205-352-6403

University of Alabama at Huntsville
301 Sparkman Drive
Huntsville 35l899
205-895-6120

Livingston University
Livingston 35470
800-621-8014

Community College of the Air Force
Maxwell Air Force Base 36112-6613
205-953-6436

Bishop State Community College
351 North Broad Street
Mobile 36603-5898
334-690-6419

University of South Alabama
245 Administration Building
Mobile 36688
334-460-6141

Faulkner University
5345 Atlanta Highway
Montgomery 6109-3398
800-879-9816

Trenholm State Technical College
1225 Air Base Blvd.
Montgomery 36108-3105
334-832-9000

Shoals Community College
P.O. Box 2545 George Wallace Blvd.
Muscle Shoals 35660
205-381-2813

Northeast Alabama State Community
College
P.O. Box 159, Hwy 35 West
Rainsville 35986-0159
205-638-4418

Bevill State Community College
P.O. Box 800, Hwy 78
Sumiton 35148
205-648-3271

Shelton State Community College
202 Skyland Blvd.
Tuscaloosa 35405-4093
205-759-1541

ALASKA
Alaska Vocational Technical Center
809 Second Avenue
Seward 99664-0889
907-224-3322

ARIZONA
Central Arizona College
8470 North Overfield Road
Coolidge 85228-9779
520-426-4260

Glendale Community College
6000 West Olive Avenue
Glendale 85302-3090
602-435-3305

Mohave Community College
1971 Jagerson Avenue
Kingman 86401-1299
520-757-4331

Mesa Community College
1833 West Southern Avenue
Mesa 85202-4866
602-461-7000

Phoenix College
1202 West Thomas Road
Phoenix 85013
602-264-2492

Scottsdale Community College
9000 East Chaparral Road
Scottsdale 85250-2699
602-423-6100

Pima Community College
2202 West Anklam Road
Tucson 85709-0001
520-206-6640

Arizona Western College
P. O. Box 929
Yuma 85366-0929
520-726-1050

ARKANSAS

Northwest Arkansas Community
College
One College Drive
Bentonville 72712
501-636-9222

South Arkansas Community College
3696 Main Street
El Dorado 71731-7010
501-862-4926

Crowley's Ridge Technical School
1620 Newcastle Road
Forrest City 72336
501-633-5411

East Arkansas Community College
1700 Newcastle Road
Forrest City 72335-9598
501-633-4480

Westark Community College
5210 Grand Avenue
Fort Smith 72913-3649
501-785-7000

North Arkansas Community Technical
College
Harrison 72601
501-743-3000

Garland County Community College
101 College Drive
Hot Springs 71913-9174
501-767-9371

University of Arkansas for Medical
Sciences
4301 West Markham
Little Rock 72205
501-686-5454

Arkansas Valley Technical Institute
P.O. Box 506, Hwy 23 North
Ozark 72949
501-667-2117

Southeast Arkansas Technical College
Pine Bluff 71603
870-543-5900

CALIFORNIA

Bakersfield College
1801 Panorama Drive
Bakersfield 93305
805-395-4301

Barstow College
2700 Barstow Road
Barstow 92311
760-252-2411

Palo Verde College
811 West Chanslor Way
Blythe 92225
619-922-6168

Southwestern College
900 Otay Lakes Road
Chula Vista 91910
619-421-6700

Canterbury Career Schools
1090 East Washington Street
Colton 92324
916-783-7400

Columbia College
P.O. Box 1849
Columbia 95310
209-533-5100

Medical Help Training School
2072 Clayton Road
Concord 94519
415-934-1947

Orange Coast College
2701 Fairview Road
Costa Mesa 92626
714-432-5773

Glendale Community College
1500 North Verdugo Road
Glendale 91208
818-240-1000

Chabot College
25555 Hesperian Boulevard
Hayward 94545
510-786-6700

Imperial Valley College
Highway 111 and Aten Road
P.O. Box 158
Imperial 92251-0158
619-352-8320

Daniel Freeman Hospital Paramedic
School
333 North Prairie Avenue
Inglewood 90301-4514
310-674-7050

College of the Desert
Copper Mountain Campus
P.O. Box 1398
Joshua Tree 92252
619-366-3791

Antelope Valley College
3041 West Avenue K
Lancaster 93536
805-943-3241

Foothill College
12345 El Monte Road
Los Altos Hills 94022-4599
415-949-7517

NOVA Institute of Health Technology
2400 South Western Avenue
Los Angeles 90018
213-735-2222

Yuba College
2088 North Beale Road
Marysville 95901
916-741-6720

Merced College
3600 M Street
Merced 95348
209-384-6000

North Valley Occupational Center
11450 Sharp Avenue
Mission Hills 91345
818-365-9645

Saddle Back College
Marguerite Parkway
Mission Viejo 92692-3697
714-582-4555

Modesto Junior College
435 College Avenue
Modesto 95350
209-575-6498

Monterey Peninsula College
980 Fremont Street
Monterey 93940
408-646-4006

East Los Angeles College
1301 Cesar Chavez Avenue
Monterey Park 91754-6001
213-265-8966

Napa Valley College
2277 Napa-Vallejo Highway
Napa 94558
707-253-3000

Merritt College
12500 Campus Drive
Oakland 94619
510-436-2598

Butte Community College
3536 Butte Campus Drive
Oroville 95965-8399
916-895-2511

Pacoima Skills Center-Lausd
13323 Louvre Street
Pacoima 91331
818-896-9558

Pasadena City College
1570 East Colorado Boulevard
Pasadena 91106
818-585-7123

Los Medanos College
2700 East Leland Road
Pittsburg 94565
510-253-4254

Porterville College
100 East College Avenue
Porterville 93257
209-791-2200

Shasta College
P.O. Box 496006
Redding 96049-6006
916-225-4841

Cerro Coso Community College
College Heights Boulevard
Ridgecrest 93555-9571
760-389-6201

Riverside Community College
4800 Magnolia Avenue
Riverside 92506-1293
909-222-8615

Sierra Community College
5000 Rocklin Road
Rocklin 95677
916-781-0430

Cosumnes River College
8401 Center Parkway
Sacramento 95823-5799
916-688-7410

Skyline College
3300 College Drive
San Bruno 94066
415-738-4251

San Diego City College
1313 Twelfth Avenue
San Diego 92101-4787
619-230-2470

San Diego Miramar College
10440 Black Mountain Road
San Diego 92126
619-536-7800

Cuesta College
P.O. Box 8106
San Luis Obispo 93403
805-546-3100

Palmoar Community College
1140 West Mission Road
San Marcos 92069
619-744-1150

College of San Mateo
1700 West Hillsdale Boulevard
San Mateo 94402
415-574-6165

Contra Coastal College
2600 Mission Bell Drive
San Pablo 94806-3195
510-235-7800

San Pedro/Wilmington Skills Center
P.O. Box 2726 Fort MacArthur
San Pedro 90731
213-831-0295

Rancho Santiago College
1530 West 17th Street
Santa Anna 92706
714-564-6000

Santa Barbara City College
721 Cliff Drive
Santa Barbara 93109
805-965-0581

Mission College
3000 Mission College Boulevard
Santa Clara 95054
408-748-2700

College of the Canyons
26455 North Rockwell Canyon Road
Santa Clarita 91355
805-259-7800

Allan Hancock College
800 South College Drive
Santa Maria 93454-6399
805-922-6966

Santa Rosa Junior College
1501 Mendocino Avenue
Santa Rosa 95401
707-527-4011

Simi Valley Adult School
3192 Los Angeles Avenue
Simi Valley 93065
805-527-4840

Lake Tahoe Community College
One College Drive
South Lake Tahoe 96150-4524
916-541-4660

San Joaquin Delta Community College
5151 Pacific Avenue
Stockton 95207
209-474-5615

Lassen Community College
P.O. Box 3000
Susanville 96130
916-257-6181

Mendocino College
P.O. Box 3000
Ukiah 95482
707-468-3102

Victor Valley College
18422 Bear Valley Road
Victorville 92392
619-245-4271

College of the Sequoias
915 South Mooney Boulevard
Visalia 93277
209-730-3727

Mount San Antonio College
1100 North Grand Avenue
Walnut 91789
909-594-5611

College of the Siskiyous
800 College Avenue
Weed 96094
916-938-5215

NOVA Institute of Health Technology
11416 Whittier Boulevard
Whittier 90601
310-695-0771

Rio Hindo College
3600 Workman Mill Road
Whittier 90601
310-692-0921

Los Angeles Harbor College
1111 South Figueroa Place
Wilmington 90744
310-522-8214

Crafton Hills College
11711 Sand Canyon Road
Yucaipa 92399-1799
909-794-2161

COLORADO

San Luis Valley Area Vocational School
1011 Main Street
Alamosa 81101
719-589-5871

San Juan Basin Area Vocational School
P.O. Box 970
Cortez 81321
303-565-8457

Morgan Community College
17800 County Road 20
Fort Morgan 80701
303-867-3081

Colorado Mountain College
P.O. Box 10001
Glenwood Springs 81602
303-945-8691

Aims Community College
P.O. Box 69
Greeley 80632-0069
970-330-8008

Lamar Community College
2401 South Main Street
Lamar 81052-3999
719-336-2248

Arapaho Community College
5900 South Santa Fe Drive
Littleton 80160-9002
303-797-5620

Northeastern Junior College
100 College Drive
Sterling 80751-2344
970-522-6600

CONNECTICUT

Capital Community Technical College
61 Woodland Street
Hartford 06105-2354
860-520-7830

Norwalk State Technical College
188 Richards Avenue
Norwalk 06854-1655
203-857-7060

Mohegan Community College
Mehan Drive
Norwich 06360
203-886-1931

Mattatuck Community College
750 Chase Parkway
Waterbury 06708
203-575-0328

DELAWARE

Delaware Technical Community College
Southern Campus
P. O. Box 610
Georgetown 19447
302-856-5400

Medical Center of Delaware
School for Emergency
Medical/Technical Training
P. O. Box 1668
Wilmington 19899
302-428-2913

DISTRICT OF COLUMBIA

The George Washington University
School of Medicine & Health Science
2300 Eye Street Northwest
Washington 20037
202-994-3725

University of the District of Columbia
4200 Connecticut Avenue Northwest
Washington 20008-1175
202-274-5010

FLORIDA

South Florida Community College
600 West College Drive
Avon Park 33825
941-453-6661

Manatee Vocational-Technical Center
5603 34th Street West
Bradenton 34210
813-751-7900

Brevard Community College
1519 Clear Lake Road
Cocoa 32922-6597
407-632-1111

Pasco-Hernando Community College
36727 Blanton Road
Dade City 33525-7599
813-847-2727

Daytona Beach Community College
1200 Volusia Avenue
Daytona Beach 32114
904-255-8131

Lake County Area Vocational-Technical
Center
2001 Kurt Street
Eustis 32726
904-357-8222

Broward Community College
225 East Las Olas Boulevard
Fort Lauderdale 33301-2298
954-761-7400

Edison Community College
8099 College Parkway Southwest
Fort Meyers 33906-6210
813-489-9300

Indian River Community College
3209 Virginia Avenue
Fort Pierce 34981
407-468-4700

Santa Fe Community College
3000 Northwest 83rd Street
Gainesville 32601
904-395-5176

Florida Community College at
Jacksonville
501 West State Street
Jacksonville 32202-4030
904-632-3110

Lake City Community College
Route 3, P.O. Box 7
Lake City 32055
904-752-1822

Palm Beach Community College
4200 Congress Avenue
Lake Worth 33461
407-439-8004

Lake-Sumter Community College
9501 U.S. Highway 441
Leesburg 34788-8751
904-787-3747

North Florida Community College
P.O. Box 419
Madison 32340-1602
904-973-2288

Miami Dade Community College
300 Northeast Second Avenue
Miami 33132-2296
305-237-7478

Central Florida Community College
P.O. Box 1388
Ocala 34478-1388
904-237-2111

Valencia Community College
P.O. Box 3028
Orlando 32802
407-299-5000

St. Johns River Community College
5001 St. Johns Avenue
Palatka 32177-3897
904-328-1571

Gulf Coast Community College
5230 West Highway 98
Panama City 32401-1058
904-769-1551

Pensacola Junior College
1000 College Boulevard
Pensacola 32504
904-484-1000

St. Petersburg Junior College
P.O. Box 13489
St. Petersburg 33733
813-791-2470

Seminole Community College
100 Weldon Boulevard
Sanford 32773-6199
407-323-1450

Sarasota County Technical Institute
4748 Beneva Road
Sarasota 34233
813-924-1365

Tallahassee Community College
444 Appleyard Drive
Tallahassee 32304-2895
904-488-9200

Hillsborough Community College
P.O. Box 31127
Tampa 33631
813-253-7000

South College
1760 North Congress Avenue
West Palm Beach 33409
561-697-9200

Polk Community College
999 Avenue "H" Northeast
Winter Haven 33881-4299
813-297-1001

GEORGIA
Darton College
2400 Gillionville Road
Albany 31707-3098
912-888-8740

Augusta Technical Institute
3116 Deans Bridge Road
Augusta 30906
706-771-4028

Carroll Technical Institute
997 South Highway 16
Carrollton 30116
404-836-6805

Dekalb Community College
555 North Indian Creek Road
Clarkston 30021-2396
404-299-4564

DeKalb Technical Institute
495 North Indian Creek Drive
Clarkston 30021-2397
404-297-9522

Dalton School Health Occupations
Practical Nursing
12214 Elkwood Drive
Dalton 30720
706-278-8922

Gwinnett Technical Institute
1250 Atkinson Road
P.O. Box 1505
Lawrenceville 30246-1505
404-962-7580

Lanier Technical Institute
2990 Landrum Education Drive
Oakwood 30566
404-531-6333

Floyd College
U.S. Highway 27 South
P.O. Box 1864
Rome 30162-1864
706-295-6339

Valdosta Technical Institute
4089 Val Tech Road
P.O. Box 928
Valdosta 31603-0928
912-333-2100

Waycross College
2001 South Georgia Parkway
Waycross 31503-9248
912-285-6133

IDAHO
Ricks College
186 Administration Building
Rexburg 83460-4107
208-356-2011

ILLINOIS
Belleville Area College
2500 Carlyle Road
Belleville 62221-5899
618-235-2700

John A Logan College
Carterville 62918-9900
618-985-3741

City College of Chicago,
Chicago City-Wide College
226 West Jackson Boulevard
Chicago 60606-6997
312-641-2595

City College of Chicago, Harold
Washington
30 East Lake Street
Chicago 60601
312-553-6000

City College of Chicago, Malcolm X
1900 West Van Buren Street
Chicago 60612-3145
312-850-7125

Columbus Hospital-Emergency Medical
Technology Program
2520 North Lakeview
Chicago 60614
312-883-6400

Loyola University
820 N. Michigan Avenue
Chicago 60611
312-915-6500

McHenry County Community College
8900 U.S. Highway 14
Crystal Lake 60012-2761
815-455-8716

Illinois Central College
One College Drive
East Peoria 61635-0001
309-694-5353

College of DuPage
Lambert Road and 22nd Street
Glen Ellyn 60137
630-942-2441

Southeastern Illinois College
3575 College Road
Harrisburg 62946
618-252-6376

Rend Lake College
Ina 62846-9801
618-437-5321

Kankakee Community College
P.O. Box 888
Kankakee 60901-0888
815-933-0345

Illinois Eastern Community College
233 E. Chestnut
Olney 62451
618-393-2982

Moraine Valley Community College
10900 South 88th Avenue
Palos Hills 60465
708-974-5345

South Suburban College
15800 South State Street
South Holland 60473
708-596-2000

INDIANA
Indiana University Bloomington
300 North Jordan Avenue
Bloomington 47405
812-855-0661

Ivy Tech State College-Southwest
3501 First Avenue
Evansville 47710-3398
812-426-1437

Lutheran College of Health Professions
3024 Fairfield Avenue
Fort Wayne 46807-1697
219-458-2446

Sawyer College-Hammond
6040 Hohman Avenue
Hammond 46320
219-931-0436

Indiana University-Purdue University
Indianapolis
425 University Boulevard
Cavenaugh Hall 129
Indianapolis 46202-5143
317-274-4591

Ivy Tech State College-Kokomo
1815 Morgan Street
Kokomo 46903-1373
765-459-0561

Ball State University
2000 West University Avenue
Muncie 47306
800-482-4BSU

IOWA
Des Moines Area Community College
Ankeny Campus
Ankeny 50021
800-362-2127

North Iowa Area Community College
500 College Drive
Mason City 50401
515-423-1264

Hawkeye Community College
1501 West Orange Road
Waterloo 50704-8015
319-296-2320

Southeastern Community College,
North Campus
1015 South Gear Avenue
West Burlington 52655-0605
319-752-2731

KANSAS
Cowle County Community
and Vocational-Tech School
125 South Second
Arkansas City 67005-2662
316-441-5312

Neosho County Community College
800 West 14th Street
Chanute 66720-2699
316-431-6222

Coffeyville Community College
400 West 11th
Coffeyville 67337-5063
316-251-7700

Colby Community College
1255 South Range
Colby 67701
913-462-3984

Cloud County Community College
2221 Campus Drive
P.O. Box 1002
Concordia 66901-1002
913-243-1435

Fort Scott Community College
2108 South Horton Street
Fort Smith 66701
316-223-2700

Barton County Community College
Route 3 Box 136Z
Great Bend 67530-9283
316-792-2701

Highland Community College
P.O. Box 68
Highland 66035-0068
913-442-6020

Independence Community College
P.O. Box 708
Independence 67301-0708
316-331-4100

Allen County Community College
1801 North Cottonwood
Iola 66749
316-365-5116

Kansas City Kansas Community College
7250 State Avenue
Kansas City 66112
913-334-1100

Johnson County Community College
12345 College Boulevard
Overland Park 66210-1299
913-469-8500

Pratt Community College
Highway 61
Pratt 67124-8317
316-672-5641

Salina Area Vocational Technical School
2562 Scanlan Avenue
Salina 67401
913-825-2261

KENTUCKY
Eastern Kentucky University
Richmond 40475-3101
606-622-1611

LOUISIANA
Alexandria Regional Technical Institute
4311 South MacArthur Drive
Alexandria 71307-5698
318-487-5439

Our Lady of the Lake College
Baton Rouge 70808
504-768-1700

Bossier Parish Community College
2919 Airline Drive North
Bossier City 71111-5801
318-746-9851

Elaine P. Nunez Community College
3700 Fontaine Street
Chalmette 70043-1249
504-278-7350

Avoyelles Technical Institute
P.O. Box 307, Highway 107
Cottonport 71327
318-876-2701

Hammond Area Technical Institute
P.O. Box 489
Hammond 70404
504-549-5063

Jefferson Davis Technical Institute
P.O. Box 1327
Jennings 70546
318-824-4811

Sowela Regional Technical Institute
P.O. Box 16950
3820 Legion Street
Lake Charles 70601
318-491-2688

University of Southwestern Louisiana
East University Avenue
Layfayette 70504
318-231-6000

American College of Prehospital
Medicine
365 Canal Street Ste. 2300
New Orleans 70130-1135
504-561-6543

Delgado College
501 City Park Avenue
New Orleans 70119-4399
504-483-4004

Huey P. Long Technical Institute
303 South Jones Street
Winnfield 71483
318-628-4342

Northeast Louisiana Technical Institute
1710 Warren Street
Winnsboro 71295
318-435-2163

MAINE
Kennebec Valley Technical College
92 Western Avenue
Fairfield 04937-1367
207-453-9762

MARYLAND
Anne Arundel Community College
101 College Parkway
Arnold 21012-1895
410-647-7100

Baltimore City Community College
2901 Liberty Heights Avenue
Baltimore 21215
410-333-5555

Essex Community College
Rossville Boulevard
Baltimore 21237-3899
410-682-6000

University of Maryland Baltimore
County
1000 Hill Top Circle
Baltimore 21250
410-455-2291

MASSACHUSETTS
Springfield College
263 Alden Street
Springfield 01109-3797
413-748-3136

Massachusetts Bay Community College
50 Oakland Street
Wellesley Hills 02181-5359
617-239-2510

Quinsigamond Community College
670 West Boylston Street
Worcester 01606-2092
508-853-2300

MICHIGAN
Oakland Community College
2900 Featherstone Road
Auburn Hills 48326
810-340-6500

Kellogg Community College
450 North Avenue
Battle Creek 49017-3397
616-965-3931

Lake Michigan College
2755 East Napier Avenue
Benton Harbor 49022-1899
616-927-3571

Henry Ford Community College
5101 Evergreen Road
Dearborn 48128
313-845-9615

Wayne County Community College
801 West Fort Street
Detroit 48226-9975
313-496-2539

Baker College of Flint
1050 West Bristol Road
Flint 48507
313-767-7600

Charles Stewart Mott Community
College
1401 East Court Street
Flint 48503-2089
810-762-0245

Davenport College
415 East Fulton
Grand Rapids 49503
616-451-3511

Kalamazoo Valley Community College
P.O. Box 4070
Kalamazoo 49003-4070
616-372-5000

Lansing Community College
419 North Capitol Avenue
Lansing 48901-7210
517-483-1957

Muskegon Community College
221 South Quarterline Road
Muskegon 49442-1493
616-773-9131

Great Lakes Jr. College of Business
320 South Washington Avenue
Saginaw 48607-1158
517-755-3457

Westshore Community College
3000 North Stiles Road
Scottville 49454-9716
616-845-6211

Montcalm Community College
2800 College Drive Southwest
Sidney 48885-0300
517-328-1250

Macomb Community College
14500 East Twelve Mile Road
Warren 48093-3896
313-445-7999

Emergency Education, Inc.
38140 Executive Drive North
Westland 48185
313-326-0920

MINNESOTA
Northeast Metro Technical College
3300 Century Avenue North
White Bear Lake 55110
612-770-2351

Ridgewater College
P.O. Box 1097
Willmar 56201-1097
320-231-2902

MISSISSIPPI
Jones County Junior College
900 South Court Street
Ellisville 39437-3901
601-477-4025

Itawamba Junior College
Fulton 38843-1099
601-862-3101

Mississippi Gulf Coast Community
College
Jefferson Davis Campus
2226 Switzer Road
Gulfport 39507
601-896-2500

University of Mississippi Medical Center
2500 North State Street
Jackson 39216
601-984-1000

West Harrison County Occupational
Training Center
21500 "B" Street
Long Beach 39560
601-868-6057

Meridian Community College
910 Highway 19 North
Meridan 39307-5890
601-484-8621

Hinds Community College-Raymond
Campus
Raymond 39154-9799
601-857-5261

Northwest Mississippi Community
College
510 North Panola Street
Senatobia 38668
601-562-3200

Southwest Mississippi Community
College
Summit 39666
601-276-2000

MISSOURI
Cape Girardeau Area Vocational-
Technical School
301 North Clark Avenue
Cape Girardeau 63701
314-334-0826

Jefferson College
1000 Viking Drive
Hillsboro 63050-2441
314-789-3951

Penn Valley Community College
3201 Southwest Trafficway
Kansas City 64111
816-759-4101

St. Louis Community College at
Meramec
Kirkwood 63122-5720
314-984-7608

Crowder College
601 Laclede Street
Neosho 64850-9160
417-451-3223

Rolla Area Vocational-Technical School
1304 East Tenth Street
Rolla 65401
314-573-3726

St. Louis Community College
at Florissant Valley
3400 Pershall Road
St. Louis 63135-1499
314-595-4250

St. Louis Community College-Forest
Park
P.O. Box 88917
St. Louis 63188-8917
314-539-5000

St. Louis University
211 North Grand Boulevard
St. Louis 63103-2097
314-977-2500

Sikeston Area Vocational Technical
School
1002 Virginia
Sikeston 63801
314-472-2581

North Central Missouri College
1301 Main Street
Trenton 64683-1824
816-359-3948

East Central College
P.O. Box 529
Union 63084-0529
341-583-5193

MONTANA
Montana State University College of
Tech-Great Falls
2100 16th Avenue South
Great Falls 59405
406-771-7140

NEBRASKA
Mid-Plains Technical Community
College
Interstate 20 and Highway 83
North Platte 69101-9491
308-532-8740

Creighton University
2500 California
Omaha 98178
800-282-5835

Western Nebraska Community College
1601 East 27th Street
Scottsbluff 69361
308-635-6010

NEVADA
Community College of Southern
Nevada
3200 East Cheyenne
North Las Vegas 89030-4296
702-643-6060

NEW HAMPSHIRE
New Hampshire Technical Institute
11 Institute Drive
Concord 03301
603-225-1800

NEW JERSEY
Camden County College
P. O. Box 200
College Drive
Blackwood 08012
609-227-7200

Union County College
1033 Springfield Avenue
Cranford 07016
908-709-7500

Atlantic Community College
J Building Admissions
5100 Black Horse Pike
Mays Landing 08330-2699
609-343-4922

Essex County College
303 University Avenue
Newark 07102-1798
973-877-3119

University of Medicine and Dentistry
of New Jersey
School of Health Related Professions
65 Bergen Street
Newark 07107-3001
201-456-5000

Bergen Community College
400 Paramus Road
Paramus 07652
201-447-7195

Passaic County College
One College Boulevard
Paterson 07505
201-684-6868

Essex County College
Westchester Campus
730 Bloomfield Avenue
West Caldwell 07006
201-228-3968

NEW MEXICO
University of New Mexico
Albuquerque 87131
505-277-2446

New Mexico Junior College
5317 Lovington Highway
Hobbs 88240-9123
505-392-5092

Dona Ana Branch Community College
Box 30001, Dept 3DA
Las Cruces 88003-8001
505-527-7539

Eastern New Mexico University-Roswell
P.O. Box 6000
Roswell 88202-6000
505-624-7149

NEW YORK
Broome Community College
Upper Front Street
P.O. Box 1017
Binghamton 13902-1017
607-778-5001

Corning Community College
One Academic Drive
Corning 14830-3297
607-962-9221

Fiorello H. LaGuardia Community
College of CUNY
31-10 Thomson Avenue
Long Island City 11101-3071
718-482-7206

Borough of Manhattan Community
College of CUNY
199 Chambers Street
New York 10007-1079
212-346-8101

Erie Community College-South Campus
4041 Southwestern Boulevard
Orchard Park 14127-2199
716-851-1003

Monroe Community College
1000 East Henrietta Road
Rochester 14623
716-292-2000

Schenectady County Community
College
78 Washington Avenue
Schenectady 12305
518-381-1366

Rockland Community College
145 College Road
Suffern 10901-3699
914-574-4237

Hudson Valley Community College
80 Vandenburgh Avenue
Troy 12180
518-270-7309

Erie Community College-North Campus
6205 Main Street
Williamsville 14221-7095
716-634-0800

NORTH CAROLINA
Asheville-Buncomb Tech Community
College
340 Victoria Road
Asheville 28801-4897
704-254-1921

Western Carolina University
Cullowhee 28723
704-227-7317

Gaston College
201 Highway 321 South
Dallas 28034-1499
704-922-6214

Catawba Valley Community College
2550 Highway 70 Southeast
Hickory 28602-9699
704-327-7009

Coastal Carolina Community College
444 Western Boulevard
Jacksonville 28546-6877
910-938-6246

Guilford Technical Institute
P.O. Box 309
Jamestown 27282-0309
910-334-4822

Wake Tech Community Collge
9101 Fayetteville Road
Raleigh 27603-5696
919-662-3343

Montgomery Community College
P.O. Box 787
Troy 27371-0787
910-576-6222

Wilson County Technical Institute
902 Herring Avenue
Wilson 27893-3310
919-291-1195

NORTH DAKOTA
Med Center One EMS Education
P.O. Box 5525
Bismarck 58505
701-224-6075

OHIO
University of Cincinnati Raymond
Walters College
9555 Plainfield Road
Cincinnati 45236
513-745-5700

Cuyahoga Community College-
Metropolitan Campus
2900 Community College Avenue
Cleveland 44115-3123
216-987-4030

Columbus State Community College
550 East Spring Street
P.O. Box 1609
Columbus 43216
614-227-2400

Sinclair Community College
444 West Third Street
Dayton 45402-1460
937-226-3060

Butler County JVS District-D
Rusell Lee Career Center
3603 Hamilton Middletown Road
Hamilton 45011
513-868-6300

Cuyahoga Community College-Eastern
Campus
4250 Richmond Road
Highland Hills 44122
216-987-2000

Lakeland Community College
7700 Clocktower Drive
Kirtland 44094
216-953-7106

Lima Technical College
4240 Campus Drive
Lima 45804
419-221-1112

Ehove Career Center
316 West Mason
Milan 44846
419-499-4663

Tri-Rivers Career Center
2222 Marion- Mount Gilead Road
Marion 43302
614-389-6347

Hocking Technical College
3301 Hocking Parkway
Nelsonville 45764-9588
614-753-3591

Edison State Community College
1973 Edison Drive
Piqua 45356-9253
937-778-8600

Belmont Technical College
120 Fox-Shannon Place
St. Clairsville 43950-9735
614-695-9500

Clark State Community College
570 East Leffel Lane
Springfield 45501-0570
937-328-6027

Jefferson Community College
4000 Sunset Boulevard
Steubenville 43952-3598
614-264-5591

University of Toledo
2081 West Bancroft
Toledo 43606-3398
419-537-2696

Youngstown State University
One University Plaza
Youngstown 44555-0001
216-742-3000

OKLAHOMA
Rogers State College
Will Rogers and College Hill
Claremore 74017-3252
918-343-7546

Redlands Community College
1300 South Country Club Road
El Reno 73036
405-262-2552

Oklahoma Christian University of
Science and Arts
Box 11000
Oklahoma City 73136-1100
405-425-5050

Oklahoma City Community College
7777 South May Avenue
Oklahoma City 73159
405-682-1611

OREGON
Southwestern Oregon Community
College
1988 Newmark Avenue
Coos Bay 97420-2912
503-888-2525

Clackamas Community College
19600 South Molalla Avenue
Oregon City 97045-7998
503-657-6958

Oregon Health Science University
3181 Southwest Sam Jackson Road
Portland 97201
503-494-7800

Portland Community College
P. O. Box 19000
Portland 97280-0990
503-977-4519

Umpqua Community College
P.O. Box 967
Roseburg 97470-0226
541-440-4616

Chemeketa Community College
4000 Lancaster Drive Northeast
Salem 97309-7070
503-399-5006

PENNSYLVANIA
Northhampton County Area Community
College
3835 Green Pond Road
Bethlehem 18017-7599
610-861-5500

Harrisburg Area Community College
1 HACC Drive
Harrisburg 17110-2999
717-780-2406

Luzerne County Community College
Prospect Street & College Middle Road
Nanticoke 18634-9804
717-740-7336

Allegheny University of the Health
Sciences
201 North 15th Street
M.S. 506
Philadelphia 19102-1192
215-762-4293

Community College of Allegheny
County, Allegheny Campus
808 Ridge Avenue
Pittsburgh 15233
412-325-6614

PUERTO RICO

Universal Technology College of
Puerto Rico
1955 Victoria Station
Aguadilla 00605-1955
809-882-2063

Center de Estudios Multidisciplinarios
602 Barbosa Avenue
Hato Rey 00917
809-765-4210

Inter American University of Puerto Rico
Metropolitan Campus
P. O. Box 1293
Hato Rey 00919
809-250-1912

Inter American University of Puerto Rico
Main Campus
P. O. Box 5100
San German 00683
787-892-3090

Electronic Data Proessing College of
Puerto Rico, Inc.
555 Munoz Rivera Avenue
San Juan 00919
809-765-3560

SOUTH CAROLINA

Greenville Technical College
P.O. Box 5616
Greenville 29606-5616
803-250-8603

SOUTH DAKOTA

Southeast Vocational-Technical Institute
2301 Career Place
Sioux Falls 57107
605-331-7624

TENNESSEE

Northeast State Technical Community
College
2425 Highway 75
Blountville 37617-0246
615-323-3191

Chattanooga State Technical
Community College
4501 Amnicola Highway
Chattanooga 37406-1018
423-697-4404

Columbia State Community College
P.O. Box 1315
Columbia 38402-1315
615-540-2548

Volunteer State Community College
1480 Nashville Pike
Gallatin 37066-3188
615-452-8600

Roane State Community College
Route 8, Box 69 Harriman Lane
Harriman 37748-5011
615-354-3000

Jackson State Community College
2046 North Parkway Street
Jackson 38301-3797
901-424-3520

Shelby State Community College
P.O. Box 40568
Memphis 38174-0568
901-528-6700

Walters State Community College
500 South Davy Crockett Parkway
Morristown 37813-6899
615-587-9722

TEXAS
Cisco Junior College, Abeline Campus
841 North Judge Ely Boulevard
Abeline 79601-4624
915-673-4567

Amarillo Community College
P.O. Box 447
Amarillo 79178-0001
806-371-5000

Trinity Valley Community College
500 South Prairieville
Athens 75751-2765
903-675-6357

Austin Community College
P.O. Box 2285
5930 Middle Fiskville Road
Austin 78752-4390
512-223-7000

Austin Community College, Rio Grand
Campus
1212 Rio Grand
Austin 78701
512-223-3030

Lee College
P.O. Box 818
Baytown 77522-0818
713-427-5611

Howard College
1001 Birdwell Lane
Big Spring 79720
915-264-5106

Frank Phillips College
P.O. Box 5118
Borger 79008
806-274-5311

Texas Southmost College
83 Fort Brown Street
Brownsville 78520-4991
210-544-8254

Blinn College, Bryan Campus
1909 South Texas Avenue
Bryan 77802
409-821-0220

Montgomery College
3200 Highway 242
College Park Drive
Conroe 77384
713-591-3523

Del Mar College
101 Baldwin
Corpus Christi 78404-3897
512-886-1255

El Centro College
Main and Lamar
Dallas 75202
214-860-2311

El Paso Community College
6601 Dyer Street
P.O. Box 20500
El Paso 79998-0500
915-594-2579

Tarrant County Junior College
1500 Houston Street
Fort Worth 76102-6599
817-882-5293

North Central Texas College
1525 West California Street
Gainesville 76240-4699
817-668-7731

Galveston College
4015 Avenue Q
Galveston 77550
409-763-6551

San Jacinto College-North Campus
5800 Uvalde Road
Houston 77049-4599
713-458-4050

Kilgore College
100 Broadway Avenue
Kilgore 75662
903-984-8531

Laredo Community College
West End Washington Street
Laredo 78040-4395
210-721-5108

North Central Texas College
Lewisville Campus
190 West Main
Lewisville 75057-3978
214-420-0089

Texas Tech University
Box 45005
Lubbock 79409-5005
806-742-1482

Angelina College
P.O. Box 1768
Lufkin 75902-1768
409-633-2548

Collin County Community College
2200 West University Drive
McKinney 75069
214-548-6710

Midland College
3600 North Garfield
Midland 79705-6399
915-685-4503

Odessa College
201 West University
Odessa 79764-7127
915-335-6575

San Jacinto College-Central Campus
8060 Spencer Highway
Pasadena 77501-2007
281-476-1819

San Antonio College
1300 San Pedro Avenue
San Antonio 78212
210-733-2581

University of Texas, Health Science
Center of San Antonio
7703 Floyd Curl Drive
San Antonio 78284-7702
210-567-2621

Texas State Technical College
Sweetwater Campus
300 College Drive
Sweetwater 79556
915-235-7300

Texarkana College
2500 North Robison Road
Texarkana 75599-0001
903-838-4541

College of the Mainland
1200 Amburn Road
Texas City 77591-2499
409-938-1211

Tomball College
30555 Tomball Parkway
Tomball 77375-4036
713-351-3300

Tyler Junior College
P.O. Box 9020
Tyler 75711
903-510-2523

McLennan Community College
1400 College Drive
Waco 76708
817-750-3617

Weatherford College, Mineral Wells
Campus
Mineral Wells Education Center
Route 4, Building 704
Weatherford 76067
817-594-5471

UTAH
Bridgerland Applied Technology Center
1301 North 600 West
Logan 84321
801-753-6780

Weber State University
1137 University Circle
Ogden 84408-1137
801-626-6743

Uintah Basin Applied Technology
Center
1100 East Lagoon Street (124-5)
Roosevelt 84066
801-722-4523

Dixie College
225 South 700 East
St. George 84770-3876
801-652-7706

VIRGINIA
Northern Virginia Community College
8333 Little River Turnpike
Annandale 22003-3796
703-323-3000

WASHINGTON
Bellingham Technical College
3028 Lindbergh Avenue
Bellingham 98225
360-738-3105

Central Washington University
400 East Eighth
Ellensburg 98926-7567
509-963-1200

Lower Columbia College
Longview 98632-0310
360-577-2304

University of Washington
Medical Technology Building
Seattle 98195
206-543-9682

Spokane Community College
1810 North Greene Street
Spokane 99207-5399
509-533-7000

Tacoma Community College
5900 South Twelfth Street
Tacoma 98465
206-566-5108

WEST VIRGINIA
West Virginia Northern Community
College
1704 Market Street
Wheeling 26003-3699
304-233-5900

WISCONSIN
Fox Valley Technical College
1825 North Bluemound Drive
Appleton 54913-2277
414-735-5713

Lakeshore Vocational Training and
Adult Education System District
1290 North Avenue
Cleveland 53015-1414
414-458-4183

Moraine Park Tech College
235 North National Avenue
Fond du Lac 54936-1940
414-924-3193

Black Hawk Technical College
P.O. Box 5009
Janesville 53547
608-756-4121

Gateway Technical College
3520 30th Avenue
Kenosha 53144-1690
414-656-8972

Western Wisconsin Tech College
304 North 6th Street
P.O. Box 908
LaCrosse 54602-0908
608-785-9569

Madison Area Technical College
3550 Anderson Street
Madison 53704-2599
608-246-6212

Waukesha County Technical College
800 Main Street
Pewaukee 53072-4601
414-691-5566

Nicolet Area Tech College
P.O. Box 518
Rhinelander 54501-0518
715-365-4451

North Central Technical College
100 Campus Drive
Wausau 54401-1880
715-675-3331

WYOMING
Casper College
125 College Drive
Casper 82601-4699
307-268-2491

Who:	Gwen Gray
What:	EMT Volunteer
Where:	Knightdale EMS
	Knightdale, NC
How long:	One and a half years
Degree:	EMT-Basic

Insider's Advice

I have always liked volunteering. I became an EMT to help the EMS squad in my area because I can be there when a lot of people can't. There have been times when my husband (a paramedic for 11 years) got out of bed in the middle of the night to answer a second duty call (because the first duty EMT was on another call) and there wasn't another person to go with him. I can drive an ambulance, he can attend, and the second duty calls can be answered when we are in town. You have to be willing to give this job your all. It will take a lot of your time whether you are a volunteer or are a paid EMT. It will also take away a lot of your sleep time because some nights you run all night. It will take a lot of learning to become a good EMT—you will take training classes every month—and it will take a lot of patience, understanding, and sometimes self-control. Most of all, it will take a lot of dedication to helping others.

Insider's Take on the Future

I do not plan to become a paramedic, but most EMTs do want to achieve this status. Not only will it allow them to practice more advanced skills, but they can go on to better paying jobs in the emergency medical services. I like being there when someone is needed. I personally don't care for blood and gore (not even those "true" emergency room dramas on television!), and so I didn't get involved for the "big adventure." It's good for anyone to take basic EMT classes because there is a lot of valuable information for anyone to learn and have knowledge of.

CHAPTER | 4

This chapter covers how to receive financial aid from the school you wish to attend, or from the county, city, or state for which you are planning to work. You'll find information on how to gather your financial records, how to determine your eligibility for financial aid, how to distinguish the different types of financial aid, and how to file your forms. You'll also find insider tips from financial aid experts.

FINANCIAL AID FOR THE TRAINING YOU NEED

Now that you have decided that landing a job as an EMT is what you really want, and you have chosen a training program, you need a plan for financing your training. That is what this chapter is all about. You can qualify for aid at several different types of schools, including community colleges, technical colleges, universities, and vocational schools that offer short-term training programs, certificates, associate degrees, and bachelor's degrees. You can often qualify for some type of financial aid even if you're attending only part time. The financial aid you'll get may be less than in full-time programs, but it can still be worthwhile and help you pay for a portion of your EMT training program.

Don't let financial aid anxiety deter you from finding out more about the many options you have for financing your training program. Take a deep breath, relax, and plunge into this chapter knowing that you can get a handle on the financial aid process during the time it takes you to finish this chapter. There are, of course, whole books devoted to financial aid, some of which are listed at the end of this chapter. Also, most schools have good financial aid advisors, who can address your concerns and help you fill out the necessary paperwork. So there is no shortage of information available to you. Take advantage of it today!

SOME MYTHS ABOUT FINANCIAL AID

There's a lot of confusion out there about financial aid. Here are three of the most common myths that need to be cleared up before digging into the financial aid process.

Myth #1: All the red tape involved in finding sources and applying for financial aid is too confusing for me.

Fact: It's really not as confusing as people say it is. The whole financial aid process is really a set of steps that are ordered and logical. Besides, several sources of help are available to you. For instance, reading this chapter will offer you a helpful overview of the entire process and give you tips on how to get the most financial aid you can. There are also resources at the end of this chapter that you can go to for additional help. If you believe you'll be able to cope with college, you'll surely be able to cope with looking for the money to go, especially if you take the process one step at a time in an organized manner.

Myth #2: For most students financial aid just means getting a loan and going into heavy debt, which isn't worth it, or working while in school, which will lead to burn-out and poor grades.

Fact: In addition to federal grants and scholarships, most schools have their own grants and scholarships, which the student doesn't have to pay back, and many students get these; it's also possible to get a combination of scholarships and loans. It's worth taking out a loan if it means attending the school you really want to attend, rather than settling for second choice or not going to school at all. As for working while in school, it's true that it is a challenge to hold down a full-time or even part-time job while in school, but a small amount of work-study employment while attending classes (10-12 hours per week) actually improves academic performance because it teaches students important time-management skills. You can attend a small college or technical school and even a university without paying a dime IF you know what to do and if you can establish adequate financial need. An example is Duaine Massey, an EMT/Firefighter from Athens, Georgia. He says that the county for which he works paid for his entire tuition and expenses. This chapter will help you apply for the financial aid you need and get you into the program of your choice without emptying your wallet.

Myth #3: I can't understand the financial aid process because of all the unfamiliar terms and strange acronyms that are used.

Fact: While you will encounter an amazing number of acronyms and some unfamiliar terms while applying for federal financial aid, you can refer to the acronym list and glossary at the end of this chapter for quick definitions and clear explanations of them all.

GETTING STARTED

The first step in beginning the financial aid process is to get a form that is called *Free Application for Federal Student Aid* (FAFSA). You can get this form from several sources: your public library, your school's financial aid office, on-line at *www.finaid.org/finaid.html*, or by calling 1-800-4-FED-AID. You need to get an original form to mail in; photocopies of federal forms are not acceptable. In financial aid circles, this form is commonly referred to by its initials: FAFSA. The FAFSA determines your eligibility status for all grants and loans provided by federal or state governments and certain college or institutional aid; therefore, it is the first step in the financial aid process and it should be done as soon as possible.

Many sources of financial aid require students to complete a FAFSA in order to become eligible for financial aid. If you are computer savvy, you can visit a Web site where you fill out and submit the FAFSA on-line. You'll need to print out, sign, and send in the release and signature pages. See the *Resources* section at the end of this chapter for the Web address.

The second step of beginning the financial aid process is to create a financial aid calendar. You can use any standard calendar—wall, desk, or portable—to do this step. The main thing is to write all of the application deadlines for each step of the financial aid process on one calendar, so you can see at a glance what needs to be done when. You can start this calendar by writing in the date you request your FAFSA. Then mark down when you receive it and when you send in the completed form. Add important dates and deadlines as you progress though each phase of the financial aid process. Using and maintaining a calendar will help the whole financial aid process run more smoothly and give you peace of mind that the important dates are written down and are not merely bouncing around in your head.

Determining Your Eligibility

To receive federal financial aid from an accredited college or institution's student aid program, you must:

- have a high school diploma or its equivalent (GED), pass a test approved by the U. S. Department of Education, or meet other standards your state establishes that are approved by the U. S. Department of Education
- be enrolled or accepted for enrollment as a regular student working toward a degree or certificate in an eligible program
- be a U. S. citizen or eligible non-citizen possessing a social security number. Refer to Immigration and Naturalization Service (INS) in the section entitled *Financial Aid Resources* that appears at the end of this chapter if you are not a U. S. citizen and are unsure of your eligibility.
- make satisfactory academic progress
- sign a statement of educational purpose and a certification statement on overpayment and default
- register with selective services, if required
- have financial need, except for some loan and other aid programs

You are eligible to apply for federal financial aid by completing the FAFSA even if you haven't yet been accepted or enrolled in a school. However, you do need to be enrolled in an accredited training program in order to actually receive any funds from a federal financial aid program.

When to Apply

Apply for financial aid as soon as possible after January 1st of the year in which you plan to enroll in school. For example, if you want to begin school in the fall of 1998, then you should apply for financial aid as soon as possible after January 1, 1998. It is easier to complete the FAFSA after you have completed your tax return, so you may want to consider filing your taxes as early as possible as well. *Do not sign, date, or send your application before January 1st of the year for which you are seeking aid.* If you apply by mail, send your completed application in the envelope that came with the original application. The envelope is already addressed, and using it will make sure your application reaches the correct address.

You must reapply for financial aid every year. However, after your first year, you will receive a Student Aid Report (SAR) in the mail before the application deadline. If no corrections need to be made, you can just sign it and send it in.

Many students lose out on thousands of dollars in grants and loans because they file too late. A financial aid administrator from William Paterson College in New Jersey suggests:

> When you fill out the Free Application for Federal Student Aid (FAFSA), you are applying for all aid available, both federal and state, work-study, student loans, etc. The important thing is complying with the deadline date. Those students who do are considered for the Pell Grant, the SEOG (Supplemental Educational Opportunity Grant), and the Perkins Loan, which is the best loan as far as interest goes. Lots of students miss the June 30th deadline, and it can mean losing $2,480 from TAG, about $350 from WPCNJ, and another $1,100 from EOF. Students, usually the ones who need the money most, often ignore the deadlines.

After you mail in your completed FAFSA, your application will be processed in approximately four weeks. Then, you will receive a Student Aid Report (SAR) in the mail. The SAR will report the information from your application and, if there are no questions or problems with your application, your SAR will report your Expected Family Contribution (EFC), the number used to determine your eligibility for federal student aid. Each school you list on the application may also receive your application information if the school is set up to receive the information electronically.

Getting Your Forms Filed

Getting your forms filed is as simple as one, two, three.

1. Get an original Federal Application for Federal Student Aid (FAFSA).

Remember to pick up an original copy of this form as photocopies are not acceptable.

2. Fill out the entire FAFSA as completely as possible.

Make an appointment with a financial aid counselor if you need help. Read the forms completely, and don't skip any relevant portions.

3. Return the FAFSA before the deadline date.

Financial aid counselors warn that many students don't file the forms before the deadline and lose out on available aid. Don't be one of those students!

Financial Need

Financial aid from many of the programs discussed in this chapter is awarded on the basis of financial need (except for unsubsidized Stafford, PLUS, and Consolidation loans, and some scholarships and grants). When you apply for federal student aid by completing the FAFSA, the information you report is used in a formula established by the U. S. Congress. The formula determines your Expected Family Contribution (EFC), an amount you and your family are expected to contribute toward your education. If your EFC is below a certain amount, you'll be eligible for a federal Pell grant, assuming you meet all other eligibility requirements.

There isn't a maximum EFC that defines eligibility for the other financial aid options. Instead, your EFC is used in an equation to determine your financial needs.

> ## Cost of Attendance – EFC = Financial Need

Your financial aid administrator calculates your cost of attendance and subtracts the amount you and your family are expected to contribute toward that cost. If there's anything left over, you're considered to have financial need.

Are You Considered Dependent or Independent?

You need to find out if you are considered to be a dependent or an independent student by the federal government. Federal policy uses strict and specific criteria to make this designation, and those criteria apply to all applicants for federal student aid equally. A dependent student is expected to have parental contribution to school expenses and an independent student is not. The parental contribution depends on the number of parents with earned income, their income and assets, the age of the older parent, the family size, and the number of family members enrolled in post-secondary education. Income is not just the adjusted gross income from the tax return, but also includes nontaxable income such as social security benefits and child support.

You're an independent student if at least one of the following applies to you:

- you are 24 years old
- you're married (even if you're separated)
- you have legal dependents other than a spouse who get more than half of their support from you and will continue to get that support during the award year

- you're an orphan or ward of the court (or were a ward of the court until age 18)
- you're a graduate or professional student
- you're a veteran of the U. S. Armed Forces—formerly engaged in active service in the U. S. Army, Navy, Air Force, Marines, or Coast Guard or as a cadet or midshipman at one of the service academies—released under a condition other than dishonorable. (ROTC students, members of the National Guard, and most reservists are not considered veterans, nor are cadets and midshipmen still enrolled in one of the military service academies.)

If you live with your parents, and if they claimed you as a dependent on their last tax return, then your need will be based on your parents' income. You do not qualify for independent status just because your parents have decided to not claim you as an exemption on their tax return (this used to be the case but is no longer) or do not want to provide financial support for your college education.

Students are classified as dependent or independent because federal student aid programs are based on the idea that students (and their parents or spouse, if applicable) have the primary responsibility for paying for their post-secondary, i.e., after high school, education.

Gathering Financial Records

Your financial need for most grants and loans depends on your financial situation. Now that you've determined if you are considered a dependent or independent student, you'll know whose financial records you need to gather for this step of the process. If you are a dependent student, then you must gather not only your own financial records, but also those of your parents because you must report their income and assets as well as your own when you complete the FAFSA. If you are an independent student, then you need to gather only your own financial records (and those of your spouse if you're married). Gather your tax records from the year previous to when you are applying. For example, if you apply for the fall of 1998, you will use your tax records from 1997.

To help you fill out the FAFSA, gather the following documents:

- U. S. Income Tax Returns (IRS Form 1040, 1040A, or 1040EZ) for the year that just ended and W-2 and 1099 forms.

- Records of untaxed income, such as Social Security benefits, AFDC or ADC, child support, welfare, pensions, military subsistence allowances, and veterans benefits
- Current bank statements and mortgage information
- Medical and dental expenses for the past year that weren't covered by health insurance
- Business and/or farm records
- Records of investments such as stocks, bonds, and mutual funds, as well as bank Certificates of Deposit (CDs) and recent statements from money market accounts
- Social Security number(s)

Even if you do not complete your federal income tax return until March or April, you should not wait to file your FAFSA until your tax returns are filed with the IRS. Instead, use estimated income information and submit the FAFSA, as noted earlier, just as soon as possible after January 1. Be as accurate as possible, but you can correct estimates later.

TYPES OF FINANCIAL AID

There are many types of financial aid available to help with school expenses. Three general categories exist for financial aid:

1. Grants and scholarships—aid that you don't have to pay back
2. Work/Study—aid that you earn by working
3. Loans—aid that you have to pay back

Grants

Grants are an advantageous form of financial aid because they do not need to be paid back. They are normally awarded based on financial need. Here are the two most common forms of grants:

Federal Pell Grants

Federal Pell grants are based on financial need and are awarded only to undergraduate students who have not yet earned a bachelor's or professional degree. For many students, Pell grants provide a foundation of financial aid to which other aid may be added. Awards for the award year depend on program funding. The maximum award for the 1996-1997 award year was $2,470. You can receive only one Pell grant in an award year, and you may not receive Pell grant funds for more than one school at a time.

How much you get will depend not only on your Expected Family Contribution (EFC) but on your cost of attendance, whether you're a full-time or part-time student, and whether you attend school for a full academic year or less. You can qualify for a Pell grant even if you are only enrolled part time in a training program. You should also be aware that some private and school-based sources of financial aid will not consider your eligibility if you haven't first applied for a Pell grant.

Federal Supplemental Educational Opportunity Grants (FSEOG)

A Federal Supplemental Educational Opportunity Grant (FSEOG) is for undergraduates with exceptional financial need—that is, students with the lowest Expected Family Contributions (EFCs). It gives priority to students who receive federal Pell grants. An FSEOG is similar to a Pell grant in that it doesn't need to be paid back.

You can receive between $100 and $4,000 a year, depending on when you apply, your level of need, and the funding level of the school you're attending. There's no guarantee that every eligible student will be able to receive a FSEOG. Students at each school are paid based on the availability of funds at that school and not all schools participate in this program. To have the best chances of getting this grant, apply as early as you can after January 1st of the year in which you plan to attend school.

Scholarships

Scholarships are almost always awarded for academic merit or for special characteristics (for example, ethnic heritage, interests, sports, parents' career, college major, geographic location) rather than financial need. The best aspect of scholarships is that you don't have to pay them back! You can obtain scholarships from federal, state, school, and private sources.

To find private sources of aid, spend a few hours in the library looking at scholarship and fellowship books or consider a reasonably priced (under $30) scholarship search service. See the *Resources* section at the end of this chapter for scholarship book titles and search services contact information. If you're currently employed, check to see if your employer has scholarships or tuition reimbursement programs available. If you're a dependent student, ask your parents, aunts, uncles, and cousins to check with groups or organizations they belong to for possible aid sources. You never know what type of private aid you might dig up. For example, any of the following groups may know of money that could be yours:

- religious organizations
- fraternal organizations
- clubs, such as the Rotary, Kiwanis, American Legion, or 4H
- athletic clubs
- veterans groups
- ethnic group associations
- unions

If you have already selected the school you will attend, check with a financial aid administrator (FAA) in the financial aid department to find out if you qualify for any school-based scholarships or other aid. More schools are offering merit-based scholarships for students with a high school GPA of a certain level or with a certain level of SAT scores in order to attract more students to their school.

While you are looking for sources of scholarships, continue to enhance your chances of winning a scholarship by participating in extracurricular or community events and volunteer activities. You should also obtain references from people who know you well and are leaders in the community, so you can submit their names and/or letters with your scholarship applications. Make a list of any awards you've received in the past or other honors that you could list on your scholarship application.

Here are a few samples of scholarships that you might be eligible for.

National Merit Scholarships

About 5,000 students each year receive this scholarship, based solely on academic performance in high school, from the National Merit Scholarship Corporation. If you are a high school senior who has excellent grades and who has scored high on tests such as the ACT and SAT, this scholarship may be for you.

The Hope Scholarship

The Hope Scholarship is a Georgia lottery funded scholarship for students who keep a 3.0 Grade Point Average or higher.

New Hampshire Charitable Fund Student Aid Program

The New Hampshire Charitable Fund Student Aid Program offers scholarships to New Hampshire residents.

Military Scholarships

Military scholarships such as the G.I. Bill are available if you are applying to the Army, Navy, Air Force, or Marines, and you may get other money for college or to pay off previous loans.

Yvorra Leadership Development Foundation

The Yvorra Leadership Development Foundation offers scholarships to members of emergency service organizations. These include volunteer, part-paid, and career personnel from fire departments, rescue squads, and emergency medical service agencies. Contact the Yvorra Leadership Development Foundation at P.O. Box 408, Port Republic, MD 20676 or at 410-586-3048 for more information.

Illinois Student Association Commission

Offers financial awards to students training to become Police Officers and Fire-fighters, who are residents of the Illinois area, and who have a GPA of over 3.0.

Maryland State Higher Education Commission

Maryland residents who are pursuing a degree in firefighting or other safety majors at a Maryland school, who agree to serve in Maryland as firefighters or rescue squad members for a certain amount of time after graduation, may be eligible for a scholarship from the Maryland State Higher Education Commission. The scholarship awards reimbursement of firefighting training up to a maximum of $2,620. Contact Maryland State Higher Education Commission, 16 Francis Street, Annapolis, MD 21401 for more information.

For a complete list of contact information for state higher education departments, see Appendix A under *Higher Education Departments*.

A financial aid counselor from Colorado Mountain College mentions:

> I am the first to get notice of EMT scholarships. I publish them in the school paper, and on the TV and radio stations on campus. I also refer students to the emergency medical services department because they sometimes have scholarships sent directly to them. Schools also offer minority scholarships, trustee scholarships, and presidential scholarships. The college will try to match you to their available scholarships.

Work-Study Programs

A variety of work-study programs exist for students. If you already know what school you want to attend, you can find out about its school-based work-study options from the student employment office. Job possibilities may include on- or off-campus jobs, part time or almost full time, in the health field or in an unrelated area. Another type of work study program is called the Federal Work-Study program and it can be applied for on the FAFSA.

The Federal Work-Study (FWS) program provides jobs for undergraduates and graduate students *with financial need*, allowing them to earn money to help pay education expenses. The program encourages community service work and provides hands-on experience related to a student's course of study, when available.

The amount of the FWS award depends on:

- when you apply (again, *apply early*)
- your level of need
- the funds available at your particular school

Your FSW salary will be at least the current federal minimum wage or higher, depending on the type of work you do and the skills required. As an undergraduate, you'll be paid by the hour (a graduate student may receive a salary), and you will receive the money directly from your school at least monthly—you cannot be paid by commission or fee. The awards are not transferable from year to year. Not all schools have work-study programs in every area of study.

An advantage of working under the FWS program is that your earnings are exempt from FICA taxes if you are enrolled full time and are working less than half time. You will be assigned a job either on-campus, in a private non-profit organization, or a public agency that offers a public service. You may provide a community service relating to emergency medical services if your school has such a program. Some schools have agreements with private for-profit companies, if the work demands your medical emergency skills. The total hourly wages you earn in each year cannot exceed your total FWS award for that year, and you cannot work more than twenty hours per week. Your financial aid administrator (FAA) or the direct employer must consider your class schedule and your academic progress before assigning your job.

If you cannot finance your entire training program through scholarships, grants, or work-study exclusively, the next step is to consider taking out a loan. Be cautious about the amount you borrow, but remember that it may be worth it to borrow money to attend a training program that will enhance your future job prospects.

Student Loans

The first step in finding a student loan is to learn the basics of loan programs. Become familiar with the various student loan programs, especially with government loans. You can get a good head start on this process by reading the rest of this chapter. To get more detailed information than appears here, seek guidance from a financial aid administrator or banking institution.

Questions to Ask Before You Take Out a Loan

In order to get the facts and clearly understand the loan you're about to take out, ask the following questions:

1. *What is the interest rate and how often is the interest capitalized?* Your college's financial aid administrator (FAA) may be able to tell you this.

2. *What fees will be charged?* Government loans generally have an origination fee, which goes to the federal government to help offset its costs, and a guarantee fee, which goes to a guaranty agency for insuring the loan. Both are deducted from the amount given to you.

3. *Will I have to make any payments while still in school?* Usually you won't, and, depending on the type of loan, the government may even pay the interest for you while you're in school.

4. *What is the grace period—the period after my schooling ends, during which no payment is required?* Is it long enough, realistically, for you to find a job and get on your feet? (A six-month grace period is common.)

5. *When will my first payment be due and approximately how much will it be?* You can get a good preview of the repayment process from the answer to this question.

6. *Who exactly will hold my loan? To whom will I be sending payments? Who should I contact with questions or inform of changes in my situation?* Your loan may be sold by the original lender to a secondary market institution.

7. *Will I have the right to pre-pay the loan, without penalty, at any time?* Some loan programs allow pre-payment with no penalty but others do not.

8. *Will deferments and forbearances be possible if I am temporarily unable to make payments?* You need to find out how to apply for a deferment or forbearance if you need it.

9. *Will the loan be canceled ("forgiven") if I become totally and permanently disabled, or if I die?* This is always a good option to have on any loan you take out.

Federal Perkins Loans

A Federal Perkins loan has the lowest interest (5 percent) of any loan available for both undergraduate and graduate students and is offered to students with exceptional financial need. You repay your school, who lends the money to you with government funds.

Depending on when you apply, your level of need, and the funding level of the school, you can borrow up to $3,000 for each year of undergraduate study. The total amount you can borrow as an undergraduate is $15,000.

The school pays you directly by check or credits your tuition account. You have nine months after you graduate (provided you were continuously enrolled at least half time) to begin repayment, with up to 10 years to pay off the entire loan.

PLUS Loans (Loans for Parents)

PLUS loans enable parents with good credit histories to borrow money to pay education expenses of a child who is a dependent undergraduate student enrolled at least half time. Your parents must submit the completed forms to your school.

To be eligible, your parents will be required to pass a credit check. If they don't pass the credit check, they might still be able to receive a loan if they can show that extenuating circumstances exist or if someone who is able to pass the credit check agrees to co-sign the loan. Your parents must also meet citizenship requirements.

The yearly limit on a PLUS Loan is equal to your cost of attendance minus any other financial aid you receive. For instance, if your cost of attendance is $6,000 and you receive $4,000 in other financial aid, your parents could borrow up to, but no more than, $2,000. The interest rate varies, but is not to exceed 9% over the life of the loan. Your parents must begin repayment while you're still in school. There is no grace period.

Federal Stafford Loans

Federal Stafford loans are low-interest loans that are given to students who attend school at least half time. The lender of the loans is usually a bank or credit union; however, sometimes a school may be the lender. Stafford loans are either subsidized or unsubsidized.

Subsidized loans are awarded on the basis of financial need. You will not be charged any interest before you begin repayment or during authorized periods of deferment. The federal government "subsidizes" the interest during these periods.

Unsubsidized loans are not awarded on the basis of financial need. You'll be charged interest from the time the loan is disbursed until it is paid in full. If you allow the interest to accumulate, it will be capitalized—that is, the interest will be added to the principal amount of your loan, and additional interest will be based upon the higher amount. This will increase the amount you have to repay.

If you're a dependent undergraduate student, you can borrow up to:

- $2,625 if you're a first-year student enrolled in a program that is at least a full academic year.
- $3,500 if you've completed your first year of study and the remainder of your program is at least a full academic year.
- $5,500 a year if you've completed two years of study and the remainder of your program is at least a full academic year.

If you're an independent undergraduate student or a dependent student whose parents are unable to get a PLUS Loan, you can borrow up to:

- $6,625 if you're a first-year student enrolled in a program that is at least a full academic year.
- $7,500 if you've completed your first year of study and the remainder of your program is at least a full academic year.

There are many borrowing limit categories to these loans, depending on whether you get an unsubsidized or subsidized loan, which year in school you're enrolled, how long your program of study is, and if you're independent or dependent. You can have both kinds of Stafford loans at the same time, but the total amount of money loaned at any given time cannot exceed $23,000. The interest rate varies, but should not exceed 8.25%. An origination fee for a Stafford loan is approximately 3 or 4 percent of the loan, and the fee will be deducted from each loan disbursement you receive. There is a six-month grace period after graduation before you must start repaying the loan.

Federal Direct Student Loans

You should be aware of federal direct student loans, which are a part of a relatively new program. The loans have basically the same terms as the federal Stafford student loans and the PLUS loans for parents. The main difference is that the U. S. Department of Education is the lender instead of a bank. One advantage to federal direct student loans is that they offer a variety of repayment terms, such as a fixed monthly payment for ten years or a variable monthly payment for up to twenty-five years that is based on a percentage of income. Be aware that not all colleges participate in this loan program.

General Guidelines for All Types of Loans

Before you commit yourself to any loans, be sure to keep in mind that these are loans, not grants or scholarships, so plan ahead and make sure that you don't borrow more than you'll be able to repay. Estimate realistically how much you'll earn when you leave school and remember that you'll have other monthly obligations such as housing, food, and transportation expenses.

Once You're In School

Once you have your loan (or loans) and you're attending classes, don't forget about the responsibility of your loan. Keep a file of information on your loan that includes copies of all your loan documents and related correspondence, along with a record of all your payments. Open and read all mail that you receive about your education loan.

Remember also that you are obligated by law to notify both your Financial Aid Administrator (FAA) and the holder or servicer of your loan if there is a change in your:

* name
* address
* enrollment status (dropping to less than half-time means that you'll have to begin payment six months later)
* anticipated graduation date

After You Leave School

After you leave school you must either begin repaying your student loan, or you may get a grace period. For example, if you have a Stafford loan you will be provided with a six-month grace period before your first payment is due; other types of loans have grace periods as well. And, if you haven't been out in the world of work before, with your loan repayment you'll begin your credit history. If you make payments on time, you'll build up a good credit rating, and credit will be easier for you to obtain for other things. Get off to a good start, so you don't run the risk of going into default. If you default (or refuse to pay back your loan) any number of the following things could happen to you as a result:

- have trouble getting any kind of credit in the future
- no longer qualify for federal or state educational financial aid
- have holds placed on your college records
- have your wages garnished
- have future federal income tax refunds taken
- have your assets seized

To avoid the negative consequences of going into default on your loan, be sure to do the following:

- Open and read all mail you receive about your education loans immediately.
- Make scheduled payments on time. Since interest is calculated daily, delays can be costly.
- Contact your servicer immediately if you can't make payments on time. Your servicer may be able to get you into a graduated or income-sensitive/ income contingent repayment plan or work with you to arrange a deferment or forbearance. In spite of the horror stories you might hear, loan officials can be quite helpful if you don't try to evade your responsibility.

There are very few circumstances under which you won't have to repay your loan. If you become permanently and totally disabled, you probably will not have to (providing the disability did not exist prior to your obtaining the aid). Likewise if you die, if your school closes permanently in the middle of the term, or if you are erroneously certified for aid by the financial aid office. However, if you're simply disappointed in your program of study or don't get the job you wanted after graduation, you are not relieved of your obligation.

Remember, too, that there are restrictions on how you can use your loan money. It's to be used strictly for education-related expenses (for example, tuition, fees, books, room and board, transportation, and so on). A CD of your favorite rock band now and then won't hurt, or if you really need a toaster oven you can get by with that. But don't use your loan to buy expensive clothing, fund elaborate vacations, or buy a new car.

Loan Repayment

When it comes time to repay your loan, you will make payments to your original lender, to a secondary market institution to which your lender has sold your loan, or to a loan servicing specialist acting as its agent to collect payments.

At the beginning of the process, try to choose the lender who offers you the best benefits (for example, a lender who lets you pay electronically, offers lower interest rates to those who consistently pay on time, or who has a toll-free number to call 24 hours a day, 7 days a week). Ask the financial aid administrator at your college to direct you to such lenders.

Be sure to check out your repayment options before borrowing. Lenders are required to offer repayment plans that will make it easier to pay back your loans. Your repayment options may include:

- **Standard repayment:** full principal and interest payments due each month throughout your loan term. You'll pay the least amount of interest using the standard repayment plan, but your monthly payments may seem high when you're just out of school.
- **Graduated repayment:** interest-only or partial interest monthly payments due early in repayment. Payment amounts increase thereafter. Some lenders offer interest-only or partial interest repayment options which provide the lowest initial monthly payments available.
- **Income-based repayment:** monthly payments are based on a percentage of your monthly income.
- **Consolidation loan:** allows the borrower to consolidate several types of federal student loans with various repayment schedules into one loan. This loan is designed to help student or parent borrowers simplify their loan repayments. The interest rate on a consolidation loan may be lower than what you're currently paying on one or more of your loans. The phone number for loan consolidation at the William D. Ford Direct Loan Program is 800-557-7392. Financial administrators recommend that you do not consolidate a Perkins loan with any other loans since the interest on a Perkins loan is already the lowest available. Loan consolidation is not available from all lenders.
- **Prepayment:** paying more than is required on your loan each month or in a lump sum is allowed for all federally-sponsored loans at any time during the life of the loan without penalty. Prepayment will reduce the total cost of your loan.

It's quite possible—in fact likely—that while you're still in school your FFELP loan will be sold to a secondary market institution such as Sallie Mae. You'll be notified of the sale by letter, and you need not worry if this happens—your loan terms and conditions will remain exactly the same or they may even improve. Indeed, the sale may give you repayment options and benefits that you would not have had otherwise. Your payments after you finish school, and your requests for information, should be directed to the new loan holder.

If you receive any interest-bearing student loans, you will have to attend exit counseling after graduation, where the loan lenders will tell you the total amount of debt and work out a payment schedule with you to determine the amount and dates of repayment. Many loans do not become due until at least six to nine months after you graduate, giving you a grace period. For example, you do not have to begin paying on the Perkins loan until nine months after you graduate. This grace period is to give you time to find a good job and start earning money. However, during this time, you may have to pay the interest on your loan.

If for some reason you remain unemployed when your payments become due, you may receive an unemployment deferment for a certain length of time. For many loans, you will have a maximum repayment period of 10 years (excluding periods of deferment and forbearance).

ANSWERS TO THE MOST FREQUENTLY ASKED QUESTIONS ABOUT FINANCIAL AID

Here are answers to the most commonly asked questions about student financial aid:

1. *I probably don't qualify for aid—should I apply for it anyway?* Yes. Many students and families mistakenly think they don't qualify for aid and fail to apply. Remember that there are some sources of aid that are not based on need. The FAFSA form is free—there's no good reason for not applying.

2. *Do I need to be admitted at a particular university before I can apply for financial aid?* No. You can apply for financial aid any time after January 1. However, to get the funds, you must be admitted and enrolled in a school.

3. *Do I have to reapply for financial aid every year?* Yes, and if your financial circumstances change, you may get either more or less aid. After your first year you will receive a "Renewal Application" which contains preprinted information from the previous year's FAFSA. Renewal of your aid also

depends on your making satisfactory progress toward a degree and achieving a minimum GPA.

4. *Are my parents responsible for my educational loans?* No. You and you alone are responsible, unless your parents or another party endorse or co-sign your loan. Parents are, however, responsible for the federal PLUS loans. If your parents (or grandparents or uncle or distant cousins) want to help pay off your loan, you can have your billing statements sent to their address.

5. *If I take a leave of absence from school, do I have to start repaying my loans?* Not immediately, but you will after the grace period. Generally, though, if you use your grace period up during your leave, you'll have to begin repayment immediately after graduation, *unless* you apply for an extension of the grace period *before* it's used up.

6. *If I get assistance from another source, should I report it to the student financial aid office?* Yes, definitely—and, sadly, your aid amount will probably be lowered *accordingly. But you'll get into trouble later on if you don't report it.*

7. *Where can I get information about federal student financial aid?* Call 1-800-4-FED-AID (1-800-433-3243) or 1-800-730-8913 (if hearing impaired) and ask for a free copy of The Student Guide: Financial Aid from the U.S. Department of Education. You can also request information from the Federal Student Aid Information Center, PO Box 84, Washington, DC 20044.

8. *Are federal work-study earnings taxable?* Yes, you must pay federal and state income tax (that is, if your state has an income tax!), although you may be exempt from FICA taxes if you are enrolled full time and work less than 20 hours a week.

9. *Where can I obtain a copy of the FAFSA?* Your guidance counselor should have the forms available. You can also get the FAFSA from the financial aid office at a local college, your local public library, or by calling 1-800-4-FED-AID.

10. *Are photocopies of the FAFSA acceptable?* No. Only the original FAFSA form produced by the U.S. Department of Education is acceptable. Photocopies, reproductions, and faxes are not acceptable.

11. *My parents are separated or divorced. Which parent is responsible for filling out the FAFSA?* If your parents are separated or divorced, the custodial

parent is responsible for filling out the FAFSA. The custodial parent is the parent with whom you lived the most during the past 12 months. Note that this is not necessarily the same as the parent who has legal custody. The question of which parent must fill out the FAFSA becomes complicated in many situations, so you should take your particular circumstance to the student financial aid office for help.

FINANCIAL AID CHECKLIST

____ Explore your options as soon as possible after you've decided to begin a training program.

____ Find out what your school requires and what financial aid it offers.

____ Complete and mail the FAFSA as soon as possible after January 1st.

____ Complete and mail other applications by the deadlines.

____ Gather loan application information and forms from your college financial aid office.

____ Forward the certified loan application to a participating lender: bank, savings and loan institution, or credit union, if necessary.

____ Carefully read all letters and notices from the school, the federal student aid processor, the need analysis service, and private scholarship organizations. Note whether financial aid will be sent before or after you are notified about admission, and how exactly you will receive the money.

____ Report any changes in your financial resources or expenses to your financial aid office so they can adjust your award accordingly.

____ Re-apply each year.

Financial Aid Acronyms Key

COA	Cost of Attendance
CWS	College Work-Study
EFC	Expected Family Contribution
EFT	Electronic Funds Transfer
ESAR	Electronic Student Aid Report
ETS	Educational Testing Service
FAA	Financial Aid Administrator
FAF	Financial Aid Form
FAFSA	Free Application for Federal Student Aid
FAO	Financial Aid Office
FDSLP	Federal Direct Student Loan Program
FFELP	Federal Family Education Loan Program
FSEOG	Federal Supplemental Educational Opportunity Grant
FWS	Federal Work-Study
GSL	Guaranteed Student Loan
PC	Parent Contribution
PLUS	Parent Loan for Undergraduate Students
SAP	Satisfactory Academic Progress
SC	Student Contribution
SLS	Supplemental Loan for Students

FINANCIAL AID TERMS—CLEARLY DEFINED

Accrued interest: Interest that accumulates on the unpaid principal balance of your loan.

Capitalization of interest: Addition of accrued interest to the principal balance of your loan which increases both your total debt and monthly payments.

Default (you won't need this one, right?): Failure to repay your education loan.

Deferment: A period when a borrower, who meets certain criteria, may suspend loan payments.

Delinquency (you won't need this one, either!): Failure to make payments when due.

Disbursement: Loan funds issued by the lender.

Forbearance: Temporary adjustment to repayment schedule for cases of financial hardship.

Grace period: Specified period of time after you graduate or leave school during which you need not make payments.

Holder: The institution that currently owns your loan.

In-school grace, and deferment interest subsidy: Interest the federal government pays for borrowers on some loans while the borrower is in school, during authorized deferments, and during grace periods.

Interest: Cost you pay to borrow money.

Interest-only payment: A payment that covers only interest owed on the loan and none of the principal balance.

Lender (Originator): Puts up the money when you take out a loan. Most lenders are financial institutions, but some state agencies and schools make loans too.

Origination fee: Fee, deducted from the principal, that is paid to the federal government to offset its cost of the subsidy to borrowers under certain loan programs.

Principal: Amount you borrow, which may increase as a result of capitalization of interest, and the amount on which you pay interest.

Promissory note: Contract between you and the lender that includes all the terms and conditions under which you promise to repay your loan.

Secondary markets: Institutions that buy student loans from originating lenders, thus providing lenders with funds to make new loans.

Servicer: Organization that administers and collects your loan. May be either the holder of your loan or an agent acting on behalf of the holder.

Subsidized Stafford loans: Loans based on financial need. The government pays the interest on a subsidized Stafford loan for borrowers while they are in-school and during specified deferment periods.

Unsubsidized Stafford loans: Loans available to borrowers, regardless of family income. Unsubsidized Stafford loan borrowers are responsible for the interest during in-school, deferment periods, and repayment.

TUITION REIMBURSEMENT

Tuition reimbursement programs pay all or most of tuition expenses for EMTs to obtain a higher certification or degree; specifically, they normally provide assistance to EMT-Basics who wish to seek continuing education to become EMT-Intermediates or EMT-Paramedics. Tuition reimbursement programs may also be available for volunteers who wish to obtain higher-level positions within their volunteer organization.

County, city, and state funded tuition reimbursement programs apply to people who work for county, city, or state funded EMS facilities, including fire, police, and ambulance companies. This benefit depends on the policies of the county, city, or state that owns the EMS facility. For example, instead of tuition reimbursement, some of these agencies give their employees a higher salary. Check with your county, city, or state run EMS facility to learn about its specific tuition reimbursement policies.

Many hospitals provide tuition reimbursement to EMTs they have hired who wish to seek a higher-level employment status. The higher level EMT can provide a more essential service for the hospital, so the hospital wants its EMTs to continue their education.

The Armed Forces provides tuition reimbursement for enlisted personnel. This tuition assistance pays up to 75 percent of college costs. Each service branch provides opportunities for full-time study to a limited number of exceptional applicants. Military personnel accepted into these highly competitive programs receive full pay, allowances, tuition, and related fees. In return, they must agree to serve an additional amount of time in the service.

To find out more about tuition reimbursement and whether or not you qualify for it at your EMS company, see your EMS supervisor.

FINANCIAL AID RESOURCES

Here are several additional resources that you can use to obtain more information about financial aid.

Telephone Numbers

These phone numbers may be of help to you when completing your financial aid application forms:

Federal Student Aid Information Center (U. S. Department of Education)

  Hotline 800-4-FED-AID (800-433-3243)

  TDD (Number for Hearing-Impaired) 800-730-8913

  For suspicion of fraud or abuse of federal aid....800-MIS-USED (800-647-8733)

Selective Service..847-688-6888

Immigration and Naturalization (INS) 415-705-4205

Internal Revenue Service (IRS) 800-829-1040

Social Security Administration...800-772-1213

National Merit Scholarship Corporation 708-866-5100

Sallie Mae's college AnswerSM Service 800-222-7183

Career College Association 202-336-6828

ACT American College Testing program...916-361-0656

College Scholarship Service (CSS) ....609-771-7725; TDD 609-883-7051

Need Access/Need Analysis Service..800-282-1550

FAFSA on the WEB Processing/Software Problems...........................800-801-0576

Internet Web Sites

Check out these Web sites for information about financial aid:

http://www.ed.gov/prog_info/SFAStudentGuide

> The *Student Guide* is a free informative brochure about financial aid and is available on-line at the Department of Education's Web address listed here.

http://www.ed.gov\prog_info\SFA\FAFSA

> This site offers students help in completing the FAFSA.

http://www.ed.gov/offices/OPE/t4_codes.html

> This site offers a list of Title IV school codes that you may need to complete the FAFSA.

http://www.ed.gov/offices/OPE/express.html

> This site enables you to fill out and submit the FAFSA on-line. You'll need to print out, sign, and send in the release and signature pages.

http://www.finaid.org/finaid

> This is one of the most comprehensive Web sites for financial aid information. They have many pages addressing special situations, such as international students, bankruptcy, defaulting on student loans, divorced parents, financially unsupportive parents, and myths about financial aid.

http://www.finaid.org/finaid/phone.html

> This site lists telephone numbers specific to loan programs, loan consolidations, tuition payment plans, and state prepaid tuition plans.

http://www.finaid.org/finaid/documents.html

> Free on-line documents can be found at this site.

http://www.finaid.org/finaid/vendors/software.html

> Software for EFC calculators and financial aid planning and advice are at this site.

http://www.career.org

> This is the Web site of the Career College Association (CCA). It offers a limited number of scholarships for attendance at private proprietary schools. Contact CCA for further information at 750 First Street, NE, Suite 900, Washington, DC 20002-4242 or visit their Web site.

http://www.salliemae.com

> Web site for Sallie Mae that contains information about loan programs.

http://www.fastweb.com

> This site is called FastWEB. If you answer a few simple questions for them (such as name and address, geographical location, associations and organizations that you are affiliated with, age, and so on), they will give you a free list of possible scholarships you might qualify for. Their database is updated regularly, and your list gets updated when new scholarships are added that fit your profile. FastWEB boasts that more than 20,000 students access their site every day.

Scholarship Search Services

If you find financial aid information overwhelming, or if you simply don't have the time to do the footwork yourself, you may want to hire a scholarship search service. Be aware that a reasonable price is $30-$50. If the service wants to charge more, investigate it carefully. Scholarship search services usually only provide you with a list of six or so sources of scholarships that you then need to check out and apply for.

Software Programs

Cash for Class
800-205-9581
FAX: 714-673-9039

Redheads Software, Inc.
3334 East Coast Highway #216
Corona del Mar, CA 92625
E-mail: cashclass@aol.com

C-LECT Financial Aid Module
800-622-7284 or 315-497-0330
FAX: 315-497-3359
Chronicle Guidance Publications
P.O. Box 1190
Moravia, NY 13118-1190

Peterson's Award Search
800-338-3282 or 609-243-9111
Peterson's
P.O. Box 2123
Princeton, NJ 08543-2123
E-mail: custsvc@petersons.com

Pinnacle Peak Solutions (Scholarships 101)

800-762-7101 or 602-951-9377

FAX: 602-948-7603

Pinnacle Peak Solutions

7735 East Windrose Drive

Scottsdale, AZ 85260

TP Software–Student Financial Aid Search Software

800-791-7791 or 619-496-8673

TP Software

P.O Box 532

Bonita, CA 91908-0532

E-mail: mail@tpsoftware.com

Books and Pamphlets

Take a look at any of the following books and pamphlets to get more information about the financial aid process.

The Student Guide

> Published by the U.S. Department of Education, this is *the* handbook about federal aid programs. To get a printed copy, call 1-800-4-FED-AID.

Looking for Student Aid

> Published by the U.S. Department of Education, this is an overview of sources of information about financial aid. To get a printed copy, call 1-800-4-FED-AID.

How Can I Receive Financial Aid for College?

> Published from the Parent Brochures ACCESS ERIC Web site. Order a printed copy by calling 800-LET-ERIC or write to ACCESS ERIC, Research Blvd-MS 5F, Rockville, MD 20850-3172.

The Best Resources for College Financial Aid 1996/97 by Michael Osborn. Published by Resource Pathways Inc., 1996.

> This book lists resources available to students, parents, and counselors—books, Web sites, CD-ROMs, videos, software—and then recommends the most useful for each stage in the financial aid search. It includes a concise description and evaluation of each resource.

10-Minute Guide to Paying for College by William D. Van Dusen and Bart Astor. Published by Arco Publishing, 1996.

> A quick, simple, step-by-step guide for getting through the financial aid process that answers the most pressing financial aid questions. Both parents and students will appreciate this easy-to-use book.

College Financial Aid for Dummies by Herm Davis and Joyce Kennedy. Published by IDG Books Worldwide, 1997.

> This fun and friendly reference guides readers through the financial aid maze by covering the major types of loans, grants, and scholarships available with strategies for how to find and secure them.

Other Financial Aid Books:

- *Annual Register of Grant Support.* Chicago: Marquis, Annual.
- *A's and B's of Academic Scholarships.* Alexandria, VA: Octameron, Annual.
- *Chronicle Student Aid Annual.* Moravia, NY: Chronicle Guidance, Annual.
- *College Blue Book. Scholarships, Fellowships, Grants and Loans.* New York: Macmillan, Annual.
- *College Financial Aid Annual.* New York: Prentice-Hall, Annual.
- *Directory of Financial Aid for Minorities.* San Carlos, CA: Reference Service Press, Biennial.
- *Directory of Financial Aid for Women.* San Carlos, CA: Reference Service Press, Biennial.
- *Don't Miss Out: the Ambitious Student's Guide to Financial Aid.* Robert and Ann Leider. Alexandria, VA: Octameron, Annual.
- *Financial Aid for Higher Education.* Dubuque: Wm. C. Brown, Biennial.
- *Financial Aid for the Disabled and their Families.* San Carlos, CA: Reference Service Press, Biennial.
- *Paying Less for College.* Princeton: Peterson's Guides, Annual.

Free Application for Federal Student Aid
1997–98 School Year

WARNING: If you purposely give false or misleading information on this form, you may be fined $10,000, sent to prison, or both.

"You" and "your" on this form always mean the student who wants aid.

Form Approved
OMB No. 1840-0110
App. Exp. 6/30/98

U.S. Department of Education
Student Financial
Assistance Programs

Use dark ink. Make capital letters and numbers clear and legible.

E X M 2 4

Fill in ovals completely. Only one oval per question. Correct ●

Incorrect marks will be ignored. Incorrect ✗ ✓

Section A: You (the student)

1–3. Your name

Your title (optional) Mr. ○ 1 Miss, Mrs., or Ms. ○ 2

1. Last name
2. First name
3. M.I.

4–7. Your permanent mailing address
(All mail will be sent to this address. See Instructions, page 2 for state/country abbreviations.)

4. Number and street (Include apt. no.)
5. City
6. State
7. ZIP code

8. Your social security number (SSN) *(Don't leave blank. See Instructions, page 2.)*

9. Your date of birth — Month Day Year 1 9

10. Your permanent home telephone number — Area code State

11. Your state of legal residence

12. Date you became a legal resident of the state in question 11 *(See Instructions, page 2.)* — Month Day Year 1 9

13–14. Your driver's license number *(Include the state abbreviation. If you don't have a license, write in "None.")*

State License number

15–16. Are you a U.S. citizen?
(See Instructions, pages 2–3.)

Yes, I am a U.S. citizen. ○ 1
No, but I am an eligible noncitizen. ○ 2
A
No, neither of the above. ○ 3

17. As of today, are you married? *(Fill in only one oval.)*

I am not married. (I am single, widowed, or divorced.) ○ 1
I am married. ○ 2
I am separated from my spouse. ○ 3

18. Date you were married, separated, divorced, or widowed. If divorced, use date of divorce or separation, whichever is earlier. *(If never married, leave blank.)* Month Year 1 9

19. Will you have your first bachelor's degree before July 1, 1997? Yes ○ 1 No ○ 2

Section B: Education Background

20–21. Date that you (the student) received, or will receive, your high school diploma, either—
(Enter one date. Leave blank if the question does not apply to you.)

• by graduating from high school **20.** Month Year 1 9

OR

• by earning a GED **21.** Month Year 1 9

22–23. Highest educational level or grade level your father and your mother completed. *(Fill in one oval for each parent. See Instructions, page 3.)*

	22. Father	23. Mother
elementary school (K–8)	○ 1	○ 1
high school (9–12)	○ 2	○ 2
college or beyond	○ 3	○ 3
unknown	○ 4	○ 4

If you (and your family) have **unusual circumstances**, complete this form and then check with your financial aid administrator. Examples:

• tuition expenses at an elementary or secondary school,
• unusual medical or dental expenses not covered by insurance,
• a family member who recently became unemployed, or
• other unusual circumstances such as changes in income or assets that might affect your eligibility for student financial aid.

Section C: Your Plans *Answer these questions about your college plans.*

Page 2

24–28. Your expected enrollment status for the 1997–98 school year *(See Instructions, page 3.)*

School term	Full time	3/4 time	1/2 time	Less than 1/2 time	Not enrolled
24. Summer term '97	◯ 1	◯ 2	◯ 3	◯ 4	◯ 5
25. Fall semester/qtr. '97	◯ 1	◯ 2	◯ 3	◯ 4	◯ 5
26. Winter quarter '97-98	◯ 1	◯ 2	◯ 3	◯ 4	◯ 5
27. Spring semester/qtr. '98	◯ 1	◯ 2	◯ 3	◯ 4	◯ 5
28. Summer term '98	◯ 1	◯ 2	◯ 3	◯ 4	◯ 5

29. Your course of study *(See Instructions for code, page 3.)* — Code

30. College degree/certificate you expect to receive *(See Instructions for code, page 3.)*

31. Date you expect to receive your degree/certificate — Month Day Year

32. Your grade level during the 1997–98 school year *(Fill in only one.)*

- 1st yr./never attended college ◯ 1
- 1st yr./attended college before ◯ 2
- 2nd year/sophomore ◯ 3
- 3rd year/junior ◯ 4
- 4th year/senior ◯ 5
- 5th year/other undergraduate ◯ 6
- 1st year graduate/professional ◯ 7
- 2nd year graduate/professional ◯ 8
- 3rd year graduate/professional ◯ 9
- Beyond 3rd year graduate/professional ◯ 10

33–35. In addition to grants, what other types of financial aid are you (and your parents) interested in? *(See Instructions, page 3.)*

33. Student employment — Yes ◯ 1 No ◯ 2
34. Student loans — Yes ◯ 1 No ◯ 2
35. Parent loans for students — Yes ◯ 1 No ◯ 2

36. If you are (or were) in college, do you plan to attend that **same college** in 1997–98? *(If this doesn't apply to you, leave blank.)* Yes ◯ 1 No ◯ 2

37. For how many dependents will you (the student) pay child care or elder care expenses in 1997–98?

38–39. Veterans education benefits you expect to receive from July 1, 1997 through June 30, 1998

38. Amount per month $ .00
39. Number of months

Section D: Student Status

40. Were you born **before** January 1, 1974? — Yes ◯ 1 No ◯ 2
41. Are you a veteran of the U.S. Armed Forces? — Yes ◯ 1 No ◯ 2
42. Will you be enrolled in a graduate or professional program (beyond a bachelor's degree) in 1997-98? — Yes ◯ 1 No ◯ 2
43. Are you married? — Yes ◯ 1 No ◯ 2
44. Are you an orphan or a ward of the court, or **were** you a ward of the court until age 18? — Yes ◯ 1 No ◯ 2
45. Do you have legal dependents (**other than a spouse**) that fit the definition in Instructions, page 4? — Yes ◯ 1 No ◯ 2

If you answered **"Yes"** to **any** question in Section D, go to Section E and fill out **both the GRAY and the WHITE** areas on the rest of this form.

If you answered **"No"** to **every** question in Section D, go to Section E and fill out **both the GREEN and the WHITE** areas on the rest of this form.

Section E: Household Information

Remember:
At least one "Yes" answer in Section D means fill out the **GRAY** and **WHITE** areas.

All "No" answers in Section D means fill out the **GREEN** and **WHITE** areas.

STUDENT (& SPOUSE)

46. Number in your household in 1997–98 *(Include yourself and your spouse. Do not include your children and other people unless they meet the definition in Instructions, page 4.)*

47. Number of college students in household in 1997–98 *(Of the number in 46, how many will be in college at least half-time in at least one term in an eligible program? Include yourself. See Instructions, page 4.)*

PARENT(S)

48. Your parent(s)' **current** marital status:

- single ◯ 1
- married ◯ 2
- separated ◯ 3
- divorced ◯ 4
- widowed ◯ 5

49. Your parent(s)' state of legal residence — State

50. Date your parent(s) became legal resident(s) of the state in question 49 *(See Instructions, page 5.)* — Month Day Year 1 9

51. Number in your parent(s) household in 1997–98 *(Include yourself and your parents. Do not include your parents' other children and other people unless they meet the definition in Instructions, page 5.)*

52. Number of college students in household in 1997–98 *(Of the number in 51, how many will be in college at least half-time in at least one term in an eligible program? Include yourself. See Instructions, page 5.)*

Section F: 1996 Income, Earnings, and Benefits *You must see Instructions, pages 5 and 6, for information about tax forms and tax filing status, especially if you are estimating taxes or filing electronically or by telephone. These instructions will tell you what income and benefits should be reported in this section.* Page 3

	STUDENT (& SPOUSE)	PARENT(S)

The following 1996 U.S. income tax figures are from: 53. *(Fill in one oval.)*   65. *(Fill in one oval.)*

A—a completed 1996 IRS Form 1040A, 1040EZ, or 1040TEL .... ○ 1   A .... ○ 1

B—a completed 1996 IRS Form 1040 .... ○ 2   B .... ○ 2

C—an estimated 1996 IRS Form 1040A, 1040EZ, or 1040TEL .... ○ 3   C .... ○ 3

D—an estimated 1996 IRS Form 1040 .... ○ 4   D .... ○ 4

E—will not file a 1996 U.S. income tax return ... *(Skip to question 57.)* ○ 5   E *(Skip to 69.)* ○ 5

1996 Total number of exemptions (Form 1040–line 6d, or 1040A–line 6d; 1040EZ filers— *see Instructions, page 6.*) 54.   66.

1996 Adjusted Gross Income (AGI: Form 1040–line 31, 1040A–line 16, or 1040EZ–line 4—*see Instructions, page 6.*) 55. $ .00   67. $ .00

1996 U.S. income tax paid (Form 1040–line 44, 1040A–line 25, or 1040EZ–line 10) 56. $ .00   68. $ .00

1996 Income earned from work (Student) 57. $ .00   (Father) 69. $ .00

1996 Income earned from work (Spouse) 58. $ .00   (Mother) 70. $ .00

1996 Untaxed Income and benefits (yearly totals only):

Earned Income Credit (Form 1040–line 54, Form 1040A–line 29c, or Form 1040EZ–line 8) 59. $ .00   71. $ .00

Untaxed Social Security Benefits 60. $ .00   72. $ .00

Aid to Families with Dependent Children (AFDC/ADC) 61. $ .00   73. $ .00

Child support received for all children 62. $ .00   74. $ .00

Other untaxed income and benefits from Worksheet #2, page 11 63. $ .00   75. $ .00

1996 Amount from Line 5, Worksheet #3, page 12 *(See Instructions.)* 64. $ .00   76. $ .00

Section G: Asset Information   **ATTENTION!**

Fill out Worksheet A or Worksheet B in Instructions, page 7. *If you meet the tax filing and income conditions on Worksheets A and B, you do not have to complete Section G to apply for Federal student aid. Some states and colleges, however, require Section G information for their own aid programs. Check with your financial aid administrator and/or State Agency.*

Age of your older parent 84.

	STUDENT (& SPOUSE)	PARENT(S)

Cash, savings, and checking accounts 77. $ .00   85. $ .00

Other real estate and investments value *(Don't include the home.)* 78. $ .00   86. $ .00

Other real estate and investments debt *(Don't include the home.)* 79. $ .00   87. $ .00

Business value 80. $ .00   88. $ .00

Business debt 81. $ .00   89. $ .00

Investment farm value *(See Instructions, page 8.)* *(Don't include a family farm.)* 82. $ .00   90. $ .00

Investment farm debt *(See Instructions, page 8.)* *(Don't include a family farm.)* 83. $ .00   91. $ .00

TAX FILERS ONLY

Section H: Releases and Signatures

92–103. What college(s) do you plan to attend in 1997–98?

(Note: The colleges you list below will have access to your application information. See Instructions, page 8.)

Housing codes	1—on-campus	3—with parent(s)
	2—off-campus	4—with relative(s) other than parent(s)

	Title IV School Code	College Name	College Street Address and City	State	Housing Code
XX.	0 5 4 3 2 1	EXAMPLE UNIVERSITY	14930 NORTH SOMEWHERE BLVD. ANYWHERE CITY	S T XX.	2
92.					93.
94.					95.
96.					97.
98.					99.
100.					101.
102.					103.

104. The U.S. Department of Education will send information from this form to your state financial aid agency and the state agencies of the colleges listed above so they can consider you for state aid. Answer **"No"** if you **don't** want information released to the state. *(See Instructions, page 9 and "Deadlines for State Student Aid," page 10.)* ....**104.** No ◯ 2

105. Males not yet registered for Selective Service (SS): Do you want SS to register you? *(See Instructions, page 9.)* ....**105.** Yes ◯ 1

106–107. Read, Sign, and Date Below

All of the information provided by me or any other person on this form is true and complete to the best of my knowledge. I understand that this application is being filed jointly by all signatories. If asked by an authorized official, I agree to give proof of the information that I have given on this form. I realize that this proof may include a copy of my U.S. or state income tax return. I also realize that if I do not give proof when asked, the student may be denied aid.

Statement of Educational Purpose. I certify that I will use any Federal Title IV, HEA funds I receive during the award year covered by this application solely for expenses related to my attendance at the institution of higher education that determined or certified my eligibility for those funds.

Certification Statement on Overpayments and Defaults. I understand that I may not receive any Federal Title IV, HEA funds if I owe an overpayment on any Title IV educational grant or loan or am in default on a Title IV educational loan unless I have made satisfactory arrangements to repay or otherwise resolve the overpayment or default. I also understand that I must notify my school if I do owe an overpayment or am in default.

Everyone whose information is given on this form should sign below. The student (and at least one parent, if parental information is given) must **sign below or this form will be returned unprocessed.**

106. Signatures *(Sign in the boxes below.)*

¹ Student
² Student's Spouse
³ Father/Stepfather
⁴ Mother/Stepmother

107. Date completed

Month Day Year

1997 ◯
1998 ◯

Section I: Preparer's Use Only

For preparers other than student, spouse, and parent(s). Student, spouse, and parent(s), sign in question 106.

Preparer's name (last, first, MI)

Firm name

Firm or preparer's address (street, city, state, ZIP)

108. Employer identification number (EIN)

OR

109. Preparer's social security number

Certification: All of the information on this form is true and complete to the best of my knowledge.

110. Preparer's signature   **Date**

School Use Only

D/O ◯   Title IV Code

FAA Signature

MDE Use Only *Do not write in this box*   Special handle

MAKE SURE THAT YOU HAVE COMPLETED, DATED, AND SIGNED THIS APPLICATION.
Mail the original application (NOT A PHOTOCOPY) to: Federal Student Aid Programs, P.O. Box 4008, Mt. Vernon, IL 62864-8608

THE INSIDE TRACK

Who:	Robert Kagel
What:	Assistant Chief
Where:	Uwchlan Ambulance, Uwchlan Township, Chester County, Pennsylvania
How long:	Two years
Degree:	High school senior; EMT certificate

Insider's Advice

The main reason I became an EMT was because my dad has been doing it for more than 25 years as a volunteer. I guess the real reason is because I love it. I have an undying passion for EMS. There is no doubt in my mind my blood has little ambulances floating around in it. I live, breathe, and sleep EMS. EMT class is generally easy, whatever class you are taking, because you want to be there. Read your material well, ask a lot of questions, see if you can get an experienced person to take you under his wing as a mentor. Ensure this person is a good teacher first. You can have an EMT god not be able to teach, and this is no good. Get a good teacher, a good mentor.

Insider's Take on the Future

I hope to return to school to become a Registered Nurse and then one day work as a Paramedic/Health Professional on a medic unit or an aeromedical service. I also hope to get a Master's in EMS administration/management and EMS education and to one day move to the top of my rank and even become a teacher myself.

CHAPTER | 5

This chapter shows how you can best succeed once you've landed your new career position as an EMT. You'll find out how to become a star performer in emergency medical services, from the qualities that are rewarded to how to move up in the ranks and interact well with coworkers and supervisors. You'll find examples of advancement opportunities within the emergency medical services as well as alternative careers such as search and rescue unit, sales, and ski patrol unit careers. You'll also find helpful advice from EMT supervisors and EMTs who are already in the field.

HOW TO SUCCEED ONCE YOU'VE LANDED THE JOB

Landing the job is one thing. Keeping the job is another altogether. Completing a training program will help you to understand an EMT's basic duties, but it won't always tell you how to manage work relationships or how to achieve the qualities that are rewarded by supervisors and senior EMTs, fire chiefs, or police sergeants. A new job can be nerve-racking. The other EMTs may be more sure of themselves and more knowledgeable than you, but if you remain calm, open-minded, and remember that you have much to learn, you will succeed as an EMT.

QUALITIES THAT ARE REWARDED

When you are being interviewed for an EMT position, the supervisors are looking for qualities in your personality and job record that will benefit the EMS team you will soon be working with. After you begin your new position, you may not immediately possess all of these qualities, but focusing on them and working hard to achieve them will help you to notice ways to improve these personal and professional qualities in your work. Read on to find out what qualities are rewarded within all kinds of EMS companies.

Be Alert

The most rewarded personal quality that all EMTs need is quick thinking skills or mental alertness. EMTs receive emergency calls suddenly and unexpectedly, sometimes in the middle of the night, so you must be able to think just as quickly. Knowing what to do in an emergency situation can be the difference in saving someone's life. If you rush through a call without being alert, you can falter in your judgment and cause greater injury to the patient. And a lack of mental alertness could even cost you your job as an EMT. Whether on an ambulance call, fire call, or police call, the choices you make can mean the difference between a victim's life or death. This is the main reason EMS companies give drug screening tests, since drugs can significantly slow your response time and alter your thinking. Since police, fire, and EMS work can be very dangerous and stressful, EMTs working in these settings need to be constantly alert and ready to deal appropriately with any situation that arises.

Be Honest

Another rewarded personal quality of EMTs is honesty. Not only do your coworkers need to be able to trust you, but so do your patients. This is the reason many police departments request that you see a psychologist and fire departments give scenario tests before hiring you as an EMT. EMT supervisors also question your honesty during an interview. They want to know what you would do in certain situations, and your answers can give them great insight into your character. Also, you cannot adequately give care if you are under the influence of any kind of drug, and patients want to be sure whatever valuables they have at the time of the accident remain in their possession, not yours. Being honest with yourself as well will help you to know that you still have much to learn, and you will keep learning throughout your career.

Be Calm

Being able to remain calm and knowledgeable about a patient's status is another rewarded quality of EMTs. If you appear highly stressed, the patient and the patient's family are going to be even more concerned about the situation than they would be already. You don't want anyone questioning whether you can do your job. Therefore, it is essential that you are calm and reassuring to the patient and any bystanders or family members, and remember that they do not need to know every terrible circumstance about the victim's injuries. No matter how things look right away, the hospital staff can change everything. Susan Carpenter, a volunteer EMT-B in Cary, North Carolina explains this further:

> Every time the buzzer and pagers go off at the station, I get butter-flies in my stomach. No two calls are ever the same. I think the day an EMT or paramedic doesn't get the butterflies is the day a mistake will happen. We deal with people's lives as well as distraught family members, and we need to stay calm. We must learn to be discrete and keep our mouths shut at appropriate times. These people are scared and need comfort and reassuring. We are there to help, not to make things worse.

Have a Sense of Humor

One of the most rewarded qualities of an EMT, whether working in an ambulance service, fire department, or other EMS facility, is having a sense of humor. An EMT/ fire officer explains:

> Since most of our time spent in the fire station is down time, waiting on calls, we spend a lot of time together just getting along. We have our daily duties, but mostly we have to be prepared to respond to any call. Many of the guys take to joking, cutting up over almost anything. If you can't take a joke, you won't like being in the midst of most discussions.

Don't be too sensitive, and realize that many times, EMTs are using jokes to help them deal with the emergency situations they are involved in daily. If you find you are taking the jokes personally, and your feelings are getting hurt, discuss this with the team members and supervisors of your squad. They may not know their humor is affecting you in such a negative way. Because members of a crew work together under conditions of stress and danger for extended periods, they should be dependable and able to get along well with all team members in a group. Another EMT explains her experiences:

> I found it hard to fit in at first, but a lot of that was that I was very nervous and anxious to learn. As a female in a mostly male world, as well as someone with no fire service background, it was a little harder to handle the guys at times. Get in the same room with four fire-fighter guys and guess at the topics. In general though, once you get over being new, it's not too hard to find your niche. Beside being able to take a joke, the qualities I see being rewarded by coworkers and supervisors include being a hard worker, reliable, safe, and willing to look for ways to get better at what we do.

Learn From Your Mistakes

Almost every EMT will tell you that an important quality to have is to be able to learn from your mistakes and not to take criticism personally. You will make mistakes on calls because no one is perfect and can think of every possible thing to do, but you want to be able to learn from those mistakes. Only experience will give you a sharper eye and keener knowledge about what to do in every crisis. Your coworkers will help you through your mistakes as well. They will be able to see from another point of view exactly what went wrong during a call. You need to always remember that you are giving a service to the community, that team members want to help you with your mistakes, and you won't be able to save everyone you meet on a call.

Remember that you are not invincible just because you saved a life. Your best quality as an EMT is your ability to learn. Robert Kagel, an EMT chief at Uwchlan Ambulance in Pennsylvania, adds:

> I have found that those EMTs who have an open mind and a willingness to listen to new ideas are the best EMTs. Be flexible. Know your stuff, and maintain a professional attitude and look. The one thing I can't stand as a supervisor and an EMT is a partner who does not maintain a high level of professionalism. You can know as much as you want; however, if you are unwilling to share that knowledge and maintain a professional look and attitude, I don't want to know you.

Have a Professional Attitude and Appearance

It is immensely important to your career and your patients that you keep a professional attitude and appearance. Having a professional attitude requires that you stay away from using drugs and drinking alcohol or putting yourself in that kind of environment. Using drugs will impair your alertness, your thinking skills, and your judgment. This behavior will put your life, your team members' lives, and the lives of the victims you are trying to help in danger, which can cost you your career and your life in an instant.

Your personal appearance is also important because it describes outwardly the type of person you are. Therefore, you should always dress in the official uniform you receive from the EMS company or department that hired you. As an EMT at an ambulance company or hospital, you will be required to wear the company shirt and designated color pants. If you are a police officer/ EMT, you will be required to wear a police uniform and whatever accessories (such as a gun belt) that you will need. If you are a firefighter/EMT, you will be required to wear a company shirt and designated colored pants while on duty, and to answer calls, you will be required to wear protective fire gear, such as a helmet, water-proof pants and coat, and water-proof boots. How you wear your uniform is also important—people look more professional with their shirt tucked in, shoelaces tied, and their hair combed.

Be a Leader

Leadership qualities are necessary for those who wish to become officers, for they must establish and maintain discipline and efficiency, as well as direct the activities of EMTs in their companies. However, leadership qualities are also necessary to be an effective EMT at any level.

When you are on a call, you need to be able to feel like you know what to do in every situation. You shouldn't have to depend on another team member to tell you what to do. If you can take charge in this manner, you have leadership qualities. You also need to be able to control the situation at the scene of an accident or crisis if there is no other type of help available such as police or firefighters. You need to be able to control a crowd for the time being or know how to calm onlookers. This takes leadership skills as well.

Showing good leadership skills will also allow your supervisor to see your potential for promotion. Leaders take the time to share their knowledge with others, they take control in traumatic situations, and they are dependable in all working situations. These qualities will help when you decide to move up the career ladder.

Interacting With Patients

The way an EMT interacts with patients is extremely important. As mentioned previously, staying calm and projecting a professional attitude can help the patient and patient's family members to stay calm as well. If you cannot remain level-headed and calm under pressure, you could seriously upset the patient more than he or she already is. That can cause the patient excess stress under already serious circumstances and could cause the patient's condition to worsen. Bystanders or any other family members who may be with the victim may also get more upset and excited if you cannot contain your feelings or words. It is important as well that you do not describe the victim's circumstance too much in detail to the family because the nature of injuries can change drastically once they have been treated at the hospital or medical facility.

If you work for an ambulance service, you may spend much of your time transporting patients. During this time, you will need to call upon your compassion for people and your professional attitude as well. Many of your transported patients will be elderly, and may need a friendly face to comfort them between locations and an open ear to listen to their voices. Your professional attitude will come in handy with those patients who may be more difficult to handle than others. The job isn't always easy or fun, but knowing you are helping others and helping to save lives will help you with the out-of-the-ordinary situations that no one can train you for.

There will also be instances where the victim or patient is rude and sometimes violent. You will need to be able to handle situations like this without being rude yourself. Many times medications and difficult situations make patients uncomfortable, so they react in a negative way. This does not mean you are to blame for their pain, nor are you expected to be able to solve all their problems, but you cannot react to them in a similar manner. Indeed, that is the time your professional demeanor is most in demand.

Interacting With Coworkers and Supervisors

The above-mentioned personal qualities are the same qualities that both your coworkers and supervisors will be looking for as you interact with them and your patients. Your coworkers and supervisors will constantly be checking your status as a new EMT, your professional attitude, and how well you learn from your mistakes. They will require you to be competent and knowledgeable, but most of all, they want to make sure you are dependable. They may have a checklist of qualities they will be looking for in you during your first few weeks or months on the job. Your coworkers and supervisors want to work with people who are like themselves—those who will go above and beyond the call of duty. This is what makes a superior EMT and a dependable worker.

While interacting with coworkers and supervisors, you should be yourself and not have a smug or quick-tempered attitude. If you have been hired as an EMT, you probably don't have to worry about your personality fitting in. However, Bob Boyd, an EMT-Paramedic and Fire Chief from Bellingham, Washington mentions that those who are in it for the glory won't last long. Remember that you became an EMT to help others by doing all you can to save their lives, and you will fit in with your coworkers and supervisors.

Your coworkers and supervisors are there to help you, guide you, and assist you at all times. However, don't take them for granted. Robert Kagel, assistant EMT chief and EMT suggests:

> The best advice I can give about interacting with coworkers and supervisors is to stay away from the politics as much as possible. You have to respect your coworkers, even if you don't like a certain quality about them. Always be willing to learn from anyone you can because no one knows everything. Someone is always teaching as someone is always learning. When interacting with your supervisors, just watch yourself. Be as flexible as possible. Also, if you help your supervisor out, he or she will in return help you, generally.

Another important aspect of getting along with coworkers and supervisors is getting to your shift on time. You need to arrive on time to receive or exchange equipment that you will need. Coworkers care the most if you're late because they are waiting for you to come, so they can go home. Supervisors care if you're late because that tells them that you cannot be depended on, and you may be late in the future to important emergency calls, which may mean the difference between someone's life or death.

MENTORS

The best resources you could have as an EMT are good mentors, people you identify as successful and who you regard as an informal teacher. Mentors are all
around you. When you begin work as an EMT, you should take advantage of your
coworkers' experiences by watching and taking in everything that goes on inside
the ambulance and at the scene of an accident. Watching the techniques of others
can help you greatly while you learn about your new job, while you get acquainted
with your new building, and while you begin to adjust to your new work surround-
ings. Mentors can help you gain greater insight into your job by showing you
aspects you may not have learned while in school. The following is a list of things
you might be able to learn from a mentor:

- Public interaction skills
- How to study for promotional exams
- What to expect in the EMS culture
- How to communicate with the chain of command in your company
- In-depth knowledge about equipment and technology used by your
  company
- Helpful tips for repair and maintenance of equipment and supplies
- What the best EMS publications are
- What conferences/classes/training programs you should attend

Every beginning EMT has much to learn about real-life life-saving. All the
training in the world can never be exactly like what you will find when you are out
in the field. You will learn most of your knowledge by watching and asking questions of the EMTs you work with. Those who have the experience know the ins and
outs of the real-life drama, and when the pressure's on, new EMTs may need the
experienced person's shoulder to lean on. Here are a couple of techniques you can
try for identifying possible mentors:

- Observe people. You can learn a lot about people by watching them. When
  asked a question, do they take the time to help you find a resolution or do
  they point you toward someone else who can help you? The one who takes
  the time to help you resolve your question is the better choice for a mentor.
  How does the potential mentor resolve problems? In a calm manner? Do
  problems get resolved? If so, that person is probably a good mentor.

♦ Listen to people who admire your potential mentor. What is it that people admire about him or her? Do the admirable qualities coincide with your values and goals? If you need to learn public presentation skills, you probably shouldn't consider a mentor who is known as a shy and quiet person who becomes tongue-tied when facing a crowd. Instead, look for someone that people describe as personable, calm in public, and who has strong teaching skills.

These are the people who will be watching you as well. As a new EMT, you will be evaluated after each call by the attending EMT in the ambulance with you. You will also need to be able to check off an ambulance without assistance—this means that a person will test you by taking certain items off a fully loaded ambulance and will ask you to tell him or her what is missing. You will be involved with on-the-job training almost the whole time you are an EMT because like EMT-Basic Susan Carpenter says, no two calls are ever the same.

Don't feel compelled to stick with the same mentor since career growth may open up new possibilities to you in new areas of specialization. If that happens, you will want to find additional mentors who can show you the ropes in the new environment. Also, any former mentors you can keep as friends may not only help you career-wise, but they can also enrich your life in personal ways.

PROFESSIONAL DEVELOPMENT

There may be a need for you to develop public relations and public speaking skills during your career as an EMT. For instance, you may find yourself interacting with reporters and public officials. You will need to know what to say and what not to say about the patients you aid—especially to reporters. If you are at the scene of an automobile accident or other type of serious accident which involved young children, you would not offer the names of such victims to reporters until the family had been notified and offered consent. These rules provide the victims with the necessary confidentiality they deserve.

In addition to public speaking know-how, you'll also need to develop your communication skills in interacting with your coworkers. For example, you will need to be able to relay all circumstances of your patient's status upon entering the emergency room of a hospital or other medical facility. In addition, you will need to fluently describe vital signs to the nurses and doctors who will take over the care of the emergency victim.

There may also be times when you will give emergency and safety lectures to others, such as to local elementary, middle school, or high school students who visit your EMS company. You may also give lectures as a guest speaker for an EMT adult education class or other related continuing education course. This public speaking experience can help prepare you for additional responsibilities and advancements in your future career. You may need to interview other employment candidates or give daily shift meetings or briefings to go over the details of the upcoming shift. You can look at all of these ways of communicating as opportunities to improve your public speaking skills.

PROTECT YOUR HEALTH

Another extremely important part of being an EMT is taking care of yourself—your body and your attitude. You can't help others if you can't take care of yourself. It's amazing how much discomfort at work comes from simply having poor health habits, both away from the job and on it. Getting enough sleep at night may be the single most important step you can take to protect your health and the health of your patients. If you're tired, you can't focus on the task at hand, and emergency victims need your full attention.

Eating a healthy diet is also an important way to maintain and protect your health. For example, eating a healthy breakfast can keep your attention away from hunger pains on your job. What you eat for breakfast or any other meal has an affect on your well-being. Eating burgers and fries for lunch and pizza for dinner has a slowing effect. Some people find that eating a light lunch and then taking a short walk immensely improves the quality of their workday afternoons.

Another way you protect yourself on the job as an EMT is to wear protective gear such as gloves and eye wear when necessary. Just as firefighters are required to wear protective clothes to protect them from fire burns and smoke inhalation, EMTs must wear gloves to protect them from diseases that can be passed through blood and masks to protect them from diseases passed through the air. You may also be required to wear a protective jacket or overcoat to keep your clothes or uniform clean.

A seatbelt will be provided in the front seats of the ambulance as well as in the back seats. It will benefit your safety greatly to wear it, since the ambulance will be riding at high speeds. If you are sitting in the back of the ambulance, you would want to wear the provided lap-belt to prevent being thrown around the back of the truck. Fire trucks and engines also provide seatbelts, as well as police cars and other safety vehicles. Your safety is important, for if you do not make it to the scene safely, you cannot save a victim's life.

KEEPING YOUR CERTIFICATION CURRENT

Re-certification requirements vary—they indicate the number of years from your initial certification to the time when you will have to be re-certified. Every EMT must be re-certified every two to four years, depending upon the state in which he or she is working.

Re-certification usually requires a certain number of hours of continuing education, demonstration of your continuing ability to perform the necessary emergency medical skills, or both. This means that you are always on top of new technologic advances, and you are continuously honing your skills to be ready for all circumstances that evolve. Your certification assures victims that you are capable of aiding them in an emergency situation.

Today, almost 80% of fire departments run by state and county communities require the EMT/firefighter to be certified at the time of employment, and the rest will require certification once you have joined the department. Police officers who are also EMTs must keep their certification current in order to be able to use Automated External Defibrillators and offer emergency medical services to victims. EMTs in all of these professions are required to obtain further education on a regular basis to keep current with new technology and skills in the emergency medical field.

Lapsed Registration

To be reinstated once your EMT registration has lapsed, you must do one of the following:

- If it has lapsed within a two-year period, you must successfully complete a state-approved refresher course for whatever certification you had last. You must submit a new application and fee and successfully complete the state approved test.
- If it has lapsed beyond a two-year period, you may have to complete another EMT-Basic training course. If you were an EMT-Intermediate and certification lapsed beyond two years, you will have to document your successful completion of a state-approved EMT-Basic and EMT-

Intermediate training course, submit a new application and fee, and successfully pass a state-approved written and practical examination.

Some EMTs may decide not to re-certify while seeking other employment and allow their certification to expire. If they decide to return to EMT work, they may seek work initially as a volunteer in a rural community that does not require certification at the time of employment, but that does require certification after the EMT is hired.

THE ROLE OF UNIONS

When you become an EMT, you may or may not want to seek out the provisions of a labor union. Depending on the region in which you work, unions may or may not play a role in your receiving the highest amount of salary and benefits according to your level of experience. Some examples of unions are the International Association of Fire Fighters, who sponsor EMT/firefighters, or the Service Employees Internet Union. These and other unions can be found in Appendix A under the heading *Unions*.

A union is an organization that combines strength and resources to organize for your rights as a laborer. There are many different types of unions for all kinds of workers. The most common types are for electricians, auto workers, steel workers, and so on. There are only a few unions for EMTs with one main branch and many local union sites in almost every city across the country. The union does many things for its members, such as:

+ Provides training and re-training programs
+ Sets standards for healthcare workers and patient care
+ Improves conditions for workers, which improves care given to patients
+ Develops leadership and advocacy skills in workers
+ Negotiates patient care contracts to address quality of care concerns
+ Negotiates increased wages, benefits, and pensions to curtail staff turnover
+ Works in coalition with healthcare reform advocates

Unions are basically a collective bargaining table and political arena. They work for the benefit of the workers and the issues surrounding them. Bill Boyd, a paramedic and fire captain from Bellingham, Washington describes his union:

> I'm member of the International Association of Firefighters Local
> 106, and I am a strong believer in collective bargaining. We have a

strong labor/management relationship that has resulted in excellent benefits, wages, and working conditions for our members. This probably would not have been possible without strong union support.

Particular areas of the country, such as the northern states, encourage the formation of unions more than other areas through their state legislature. In the North, many ambulance services and fire departments require their employees to join a particular union in order to work for them. In many of these locations, unions are considered to be highly esteemed traditions. However, there are not as many union coalitions in the southern states, which have legislature called the "right to work" that makes it harder for unions to organize. Also, many small fire departments and ambulance services may not be affiliated with a particular union. If you join an EMS company that is collectively affiliated with a union but does not require membership, you may want to consider joining the union anyway, since it would be to your benefit.

ADVANCEMENT OPPORTUNITIES

Many times, an EMT-Basic must get additional training to advance in rank or salary. You have to determine what is important to you when considering advancement opportunities, so your career choices fit into an overall plan. However, promotion can only happen if you do your best at the commitment you've made with your entry-level position as an EMT-Basic and at receiving proper continuing education if needed. Before you ask for a promotion, show your employer or supervisor that you have dedicated yourself to your current position, you've performed well, your attendance is satisfactory, you've been cooperative and flexible, and you have gained the necessary training.

Promote Yourself to a Better Job

You can promote yourself to a better job by getting hired as an EMT in another EMS company that offers you more advancement opportunities. There are several reasons why you might want to apply to another EMS company. Even if it's a lateral move, you can get any one or more of the added benefits from a move:

- Better pay
- Better health benefits or work schedule
- Better training programs

- Better EMS equipment
- Better camaraderie with coworkers and supervisors
- More room for advancement

Of course, if you land your first job in a great EMS company that has a lot of benefits and advancement opportunities, then you're all set. You can focus on learning all you can and on applying yourself for future promotional opportunities or career challenges in related areas at that company. If you decide to seek advancement in the EMS field, there are several things you can do to prepare for a promotion.

How to Prepare for a Promotion

Many experienced EMTs study regularly to improve their job performance and to prepare for promotion examinations. Today, EMTs at all levels need more training to operate increasingly sophisticated equipment and to deal safely with the greater hazards associated with emergency situations, such as fighting fires, controlling criminals, and stabilizing severely injured victims.

To progress to higher level positions, EMTs must acquire expertise in the most advanced EMT equipment and lifesaving techniques and emergency procedures, writing, public speaking, management and budgeting procedures, and labor relations. This is true for EMT-Basics who want to become EMT-Intermediates or paramedics. This is also true for firefighter/EMTs who want to be promoted within the fire department or police officer/EMTs who want to be promoted within the police department.

Taking the Promotional Exam

Once you've decided you really want to get a particular promotion, you will need to set up a plan for obtaining that goal. Several things can help your chances of scoring high on a promotion exam. Here are a few of them:

- Set priorities on what material to study. You can't possibly learn every detail about the job you want to obtain, so focus on the most important aspects. If you don't do this step, you can easily get bogged down in wading through details that are not going to be tested on the promotional examination.
- Get an idea of what will be on the promotional examination. You can ask people who have already taken the exam what areas were emphasized and

what books they recommend you study to prepare for the exam. You may be able to get old tests that have been published for students to review relevant material. Or you may be fortunate enough to get a suggested reading list along with the exam materials in some departments, although this is rare.

♦ Study test preparation books to find out or brush up on the skills needed to succeed on promotional exams. For example, look up information on how to handle test anxiety, how to score the highest possible on multiple-choice questions, and how to take tests within specific time limits.

♦ Make a study schedule several months before the exam and stick to it. Allow sufficient time each day for studying a section of material, and don't forget to preview and review the material you study each day. One study method is to create flash cards and test yourself on key concepts and questions that you think may appear on the test.

♦ Find out if your EMS company uses assessment centers to test practical, hands-on aspects of the job you are applying for. If so, talk to people who have gone through the assessment center to get their advice on how you can prepare for this segment of the process. You should also ask if you can tour the assessment facility to get an idea of what equipment is used to test you.

Promotion to EMT-Paramedic

Many hospitals want EMTs to be paramedics or be enrolled in paramedic training because EMT-Paramedics can perform more advanced pre-hospital procedures, such as administering drugs intravenously, performing endotracheal intubations, and operating complicated life support equipment. This career advancement can raise your salary from $10,000 to $15,000 a year. Opportunities for EMT-Basics or EMT-Intermediates who receive this advanced training while working in small ambulance services, fire departments, or police departments often depend on the status of senior EMTs in the particular department or on turnover rates. For example, in many small emergency medical facilities, EMTs must wait until someone transfers, retires, or dies before they get a promotion.

Turnover rates for EMT-Basics and EMT-Intermediates are higher in the private service sector than in the public service sector due to stressful working conditions, limited advancement potential, and modest pay and benefits. Therefore, opportunities for entry-level EMTs are better in hospitals and private ambulance services where pay and benefits are usually lower. Many EMTs get their start in the private sector and then move into the public sector once they have achieved a certain level of experience.

Take a look at this example of a recent job posting for an EMT-Paramedic to get an idea of what advancement opportunities are available in your future career.

Job Summary:	EMT-Paramedic
Education:	Completion of EMT-Paramedic certificate courses or an EMT-Paramedic Associate degree
Licensure:	Current state or NREMT certification as EMT-Paramedic
Experience:	At least one year as a street paramedic
Skills:	Applicant must possess skills related to experience as EMT-Paramedic

Essential Physical and Mental Functions and Environmental Conditions:

Applicant must be able to communicate effectively with patients, dispatchers, and medical facility staff.

Applicant must be able to care adequately for patients under the guidelines of the title EMT-Paramedic.

Applicant must be able to handle traumatic situations calmly and efficiently and remain in control under extreme duress.

Applicant must provide a clean driving record, background record, drug screen, and excellent physical examination.

Promotion in the Fire Department

Opportunities for promotion are good in most fire departments. As EMT/ firefighters gain expertise, they may advance to a higher rank. The line of promotion is usually to engineer, lieutenant, captain, battalion chief, assistant chief, deputy chief, and finally, to chief. For EMT-Basics, it may be to the EMT-Intermediate or EMT-Paramedic position. Advancement generally depends upon written examination scores, job performance, interviews, and seniority. Increasingly, fire departments are using assessment centers—which simulate a variety of actual job performance tasks—to screen for the best candidates for promotion.

Associate and bachelor's degrees are available in fire science as well as EMT-Paramedic. Many fire departments now require a bachelor's degree—preferably in fire science, public administration, or a related field—for promotion to positions higher than battalion chief. Some departments also require a master's degree, as well as executive fire officer certification from the National Fire Academy or state chief officer certification, for the position of fire chief.

Take a look at this example of a recent job posting for a Firefighter II/ Paramedic to get an idea of what advancement opportunities are available in the firefighting emergency medical services field.

Job Summary:	Firefighter II/Paramedic
Education:	EMT-Paramedic certificate and Firefighter II certificate
Licensure:	Current state or NREMT EMT-Paramedic certification
Experience:	Three years as a professional firefighter
Skills:	Skills must be related to firefighting and EMT-Paramedic status

Essential Physical and Mental Functions and Environmental Conditions:

Qualified candidates must be between the ages of 21 and 35.

Applicants must be able to communicate effectively with fire officers, dispatchers, medical professionals, and accident victims.

Applicants must be able to complete necessary fire drills, drive emergency vehicles, and use necessary fire and EMT equipment.

Promotion in the Police Department

Police officers usually become eligible for promotion after a probationary period ranging from six months to three years. Promotion may consist of moving from police officer I to police officer II and so on before moving up to a corporal, sergeant, lieutenant, and captain. These promotions are usually made according to a candidate's position on a promotion list, as determined by written promotion examination scores, referral, and on-the-job performance.

Police departments are encouraging applicants to take post-secondary school training in law enforcement. Required continued training and refresher courses aid officers in improving their job performance.

Take a look at this example of a recent job posting for Police officer/ Paramedic to get an idea of what advancement opportunities are available in emergency medical services in police departments.

Job Summary:	Police Officer/Paramedic
Education:	Completed Police officer academy training courses; Completed EMT-Paramedic certificate course or associate degree course
Licensure:	Current state or NREMT EMT certification
Experience:	At least two years as a street paramedic
Skills:	Applicant must possess skills related to the police officer and the EMT-Paramedic

Essential Physical and Mental Functions and Environmental Conditions:

Applicant must be at least 21 years of age, in excellent physical and mental health, and remain in control under extreme duress.

Applicant must be able to recall details of the scene of crimes, preserve evidence as appropriate, and secure the safety of the emergency scene using investigation and identification techniques.

Applicant must be able to provide emergency relief to victims of emergencies, utilize necessary equipment, and cooperate with local EMS agencies.

Applicants must be able to communicate with victims, bystanders, and dispatchers, and provide crowd control.

RELATED CAREER OPTIONS

There are many different career options for EMTs whether they progress to EMT-Paramedics or they decide to go on to different professions within related areas. In some departments, you can be promoted into many different positions, but you can also find alternative employment that you may never have thought of. Here is a list of several careers that are related to or use the experience gained in emergency medical services.

EMT Dispatcher

EMTs can, with further training, become *EMT dispatchers*. As discussed in chapter one, the dispatcher receives the call for help, sends out the appropriate medical resource, remains the link between the emergency vehicle and the medical facility throughout the situation, and relays any requests for special assistance to the hospital. Dispatchers are crucial in helping the EMT get to the scene of an accident. Dispatchers also play a key role in helping to save the lives of medical emergency victims. They may need to give lifesaving instructions to bystanders or family members while the victims are awaiting an ambulance or other emergency units.

Firefighter

As discussed in chapter one, EMTs can also be *firefighters*. EMTs who want to become firefighters must complete required firefighting training first. Firefighters who want to become EMTs must complete the EMT-Basic course. Firefighter/EMTs may also become part-time volunteers for other related occupations such as search and rescue teams.

Promotions you could achieve after becoming a Firefighter/EMT include eventually becoming a Firefighter/Paramedic, an engineer, a lieutenant, a captain, a battalion chief, an assistant chief, a deputy chief, or a fire chief. Advancement usually depends on scores achieved on a written promotion examination, job performance, interviews, and seniority.

Police Officer

EMT/police officers are discussed in chapter one as well. EMTs who want to become *police officers* must complete required police officer training first. Police officers who want to become EMTs must complete the EMT-Basic course. Police officer/ EMTs may also become part-time volunteers for local police or sheriff search and rescue teams.

EMT/police officers can be further promoted to corporal, sergeant, lieutenant, and captain, or they can become detectives or special agents. They can also become instructors themselves, who train other police officer candidates.

Instructor

EMT-Paramedics can become *instructors* of EMT courses, teaching others their skills and sharing their years of experience. You can become an instructor at whatever level of EMT training you achieve, as Jeanine Hoffman, EMT-Basic and class-coordinator and primary instructor at Harrisburg Community College in Pennsylvania explained in chapter one. A college or technical institute you wish to teach at may or may not have special requirements, such as possession of an associate or bachelor's degree or a certain number of years of experience; this will depend on the institution's requirements. You may also teach classes outside of a school or technical institute atmosphere. For example, many EMS companies give CPR, first aid, and other types of safety classes. EMS companies may also be the site of EMT-Basic and EMT-Intermediate refresher courses. You will most likely be required to achieve a certain level of certification before you can teach that level.

For example, teaching a paramedic class requires you to have an associate degree as an EMT-Paramedic or higher and a certain number of years experience.

Your level of salary after you become an instructor will depend greatly on your academic credentials, experience, and the region of the country in which you are teaching. You may become a full-time- or part-time instructor, teaching while working or volunteering as an EMT. Whatever path you choose, becoming an instructor is a great way to pass on the wealth of experience and knowledge you gain as an EMT.

Flight Paramedic

EMT-Paramedics can become *flight paramedics* for emergency air medical transport, and those with a pilot's license can fly the small planes or helicopters used for the transport. Airplanes and helicopters routinely fly critical care patients from one medical facility to another, and they also move patients who may be unable to fly on commercial airlines for any number of reasons. Flight paramedicine often is an expanded role for paramedics. It can be challenging, rewarding, and highly competitive.

For more information on becoming a flight paramedic contact the National Flight Paramedic's Association at 7136 S. Yale Ave., Suite 300, Tulsa, OK 74136, or call (800) 381-NFPA.

Search & Rescue Unit

EMTs can train to work on *search and rescue units* that are all-terrain, all-weather, ground, air, water, mountain search and rescue teams, and disaster relief teams. Unit members are trained in wilderness penetration and movement, land navigation, downed aircraft reconnaissance, lost-person search techniques, tracking strategies, wilderness rescue skills, team organization, water crossing, and wildfire suppression. These teams may also use search dogs to find victims.

Each team member is trained at a minimum as a first responder or EMT-Basic, depending upon the requirements of the individual search & rescue team. Members are also certified in wildfire control, and units are capable of fielding certified divers for water search and rescue. Each geographical area may have a different kind of team, depending on the region's predominant land description. Search and rescue units in mountainous regions perform more cliff rescues and have more technical rope teams, whereas river regions require search and rescue teams who are trained in water rescue. Appropriate training is available in the different regions.

For more information on how to get hired and excel on search & rescue teams, contact the National Association for Search & Rescue at 4500 Southgate Place, Suite 100, Chantilly, VA 20151-1714, or call them at (703) 222-6277. Another resource you can contact is the National Institute for Urban Search & Rescue at P. O. Box 90909, Santa Barbara, CA 93190, or call (805) 569-5066.

American Red Cross Worker

American Red Cross workers provide relief to victims of disasters and help people prevent, prepare for, and respond to emergencies. The American Red Cross provides many services, such as:

- ♦ Food and shelter to victims of disasters
- ♦ Services to members of the armed forces and their families
- ♦ Instruction in first aid and water safety
- ♦ HIV/AIDS education
- ♦ Home nursing
- ♦ Blood and tissue banking services
- ♦ International aid

The work of the Red Cross is made possible by more than 1.5 million volunteers across the country, 30,000 staff members, and the financial contributions of the American people. There are 50 volunteers to every paid staff member. The Red Cross is committed to making a positive difference by improving the quality of human life, enhancing self-reliance and concern for others, and helping people avoid, prepare for, and cope with emergencies.

For more information about the American Red Cross and how you can volunteer, contact the American Red Cross at its National Headquarters at 8111 Gatehouse Rd., Galls Church, VA 22042 or call (202) 737-8300.

Ski Patrol Unit

EMTs can also train to work on *ski patrol units* that serve skiers, hikers, snowboarders, and other snow- and mountain-stranded victims. Patrollers in ski patrol units are well-versed in various special rescue techniques including toboggan handling, chairlift evacuation, technical rope rescues, avalanche control and rescue, and out-of-area search & rescue.

Ski patrollers are usually certified as Outdoor Emergency Care Technicians. The requirement for obtaining this level of certification is completion of the EMT-Basic coursework with an emphasis on patrolling the snow and mountain environment. Many colleges that are located close to geographic areas that get a lot of snow offer a course entitled *Ski Area Operations* as well as EMT and First Responder courses. An example of such a college is the Colorado Mountain College, and it has campuses all over the state of Colorado.

Ski patrol units also offer safety programs to winter recreation participants. Such programs offer survival skills in topics such as emergency shelter construction, navigation by map, winter route planning, emergency equipment repair, and winter first aid.

For more information on ski patrol units, write to the National Ski Patrol at 133 South Van Gordon St., Suite 100, Lakewood, CO 80228, or call them at (303) 988-1111.

Nurse

EMTs also enter the *nursing* field, moving from medical transport to the hospital to work as Registered Nurses (RN), Licensed Practical Nurses (LPN), and nurse's aides, where patient care is less traumatic and short-term and is more personal and long-term. EMT-Basics and EMT-Intermediates usually require more training to become a registered nurse because becoming an RN requires an associate degree or higher. However, most EMT-Paramedics can switch over to nursing more easily, since they probably already obtained an associate degree. Becoming a nurse's aide would require almost no further training for any level EMT.

Many times EMTs feel that the stress of working in emergency services is taking a toll on their health, and they see a more calm and attractive environment in being a hospital or staff nurse caring for patients.

For more information about becoming a nurse, contact the American Nurses Association at 600 Maryland Ave. SW, Washington, DC 20024-2571, or call them at (800) 274-4ANA. Another association you can contact for more information is the National League for Nursing at 350 Hudson St., New York, NY 10014, or call (800) 669-1656.

Lifeguard

Lifeguard responsibilities include water rescue of swimmers and surfers, boater rescue up to three miles offshore, boat fire suppression, coastal cliff rescue, underwater search and rescue, missing persons, and other such related emergencies. Included within the lifeguard service is the *boating safety unit* that provides harbor patrol and ocean rescue service for boaters. Lifeguards assigned to the boating safety unit enforce boating regulations, and they handle issuance of boat mooring permits and long-term boat beaching permits. During periods of flooding, the lifeguard *river rescue team* handles rescues. The *dive rescue team* handles underwater search and recovery. Administrative positions may include a Lifeguard Chief, several Lieutenants and Sergeants, and an office staff.

Usually, all full-time lifeguards are Emergency Medical Technicians. Hourly lifeguards are certified by a minimum of American Red Cross Emergency Response. River rescue teams are certified at the instructor level. Dive rescue team members are certified as Advanced Scuba Divers and Dive Rescue Specialists. Lifeguards who work in the boating safety unit are fully equipped and trained to operate the lifeguard service's fire boats, and they also suppress fires.

For more career information on becoming a lifeguard, contact the United States Lifesaving Association at P. O. Box 322, Avon-by-the-Sea, NJ 07717, or call them at (800) FOR-USLA.

Sales Representative

EMT-Paramedics can also become *sales representatives*, selling emergency medical equipment to EMS facilities. Manufacturers' and wholesale sales representatives spend much of their time traveling to and visiting with prospective buyers and current clients. During a sales call, they discuss the customers' needs and suggest how their merchandise or services can meet those needs. They may show samples or catalogs that describe items their company stocks and inform customers about prices, availability, and how their products can save money and improve productivity. They also take orders and resolve any problems or complaints with the merchandise.

Sales representatives usually cover large territories, and they do considerable traveling. They may cover several states and be away from home for days or weeks at a time. However, they do have the freedom to determine their own schedule. Sales representatives also attend EMS trade shows to keep abreast of new merchandise and the changing needs of EMS customers.

Sales earnings vary significantly and can be based on commission and salary or commission and bonuses. Bonuses can be based on individual performance, on all workers in a company, or on the company's performance. Sales representatives are usually reimbursed for expenses such as transportation costs, meals, hotels, and entertaining customers. They often receive benefits such as health and life insurance, a pension plan, vacation and sick leave, personal use of a company car, and frequent flyer mileage. Some companies offer incentives such as free vacation trips or gifts for outstanding sales representatives.

Software Engineers

Some EMTs have become *software engineers* since they know firsthand what kind of software is needed in an EMS company. For example, an EMT from Georgia created mapping software that is used at several hospitals and EMS facilities in the area. The software is used to more quickly locate the scene of an accident, as well as to locate the ambulances that are out on the road already. For some emergencies, it may be quicker to send an ambulance that is already out on the road returning from another call than to issue a new departure from the hospital or EMS facility. The mapping software is a more efficient way of viewing a map; it focuses on the scene of the emergency and the surrounding streets, and it offers suggestions on the best way to get there.

Software engineers are involved in the design and development of software systems that control and automate manufacturing, business, and management processes. They also may design and develop both packaged and systems software or be involved in creating custom software applications for clients.

Employers generally look for people who are familiar with programming languages and who have a broad knowledge of and experience with computer systems and technologies. Successful software engineers also have strong problem-solving and analysis skills and good interpersonal skills. Taking courses in computer programming or systems design can offer you preparation for a job in this field. If you have a related background in the industry in which the job is located, it will give you a competitive edge.

For more information on becoming a software engineer, you can contact a company like EMT Software Inc. at 119 N. Commercial St., Bellingham, WA 98225, or call (800) 698-1727.

ACHIEVE SUCCESS

Once you've landed the job you've worked so hard to get, do your best to make it worth your time and energy. Put your best foot forward, and really prove to your boss that you appreciate the chance to succeed. Make positive relationships with coworkers, share ideas and common interests, and be friendly at all times. Get to work on time, be efficient, and even when you're having a bad day, smile, and don't take your bad feelings out on anyone else.

Find someone within your work environment to take you under his or her wing. Focus on maintaining a good work record after you've proven your capabilities during your probationary period. Show everyone your best, and you will have the chance to succeed and move on to larger environments and higher levels of pay. Also, remember the EMT oath:

The EMT Oath

Be it pledged as an Emergency Medical Technician, I will honor the physical and judicial laws of God and man. I will follow that regimen which, according to my ability and judgment, I consider for the benefit of patients and abstain from whatever is deleterious and mischievous, nor shall I suggest any such counsel. Into whatever homes I enter, I will go into them for the benefit of only the sick and injured, never revealing what I see or hear in the lives of men unless required by law.

I shall also share my medical knowledge with those who may benefit from what I have learned. I will serve unselfishly and continuously in order to help make a better world for all mankind.

While I continue to keep this oath unviolated, may it be granted to me to enjoy life, and the practice of the art, respected by all men, in all times. Should I trespass or violate this oath, may the reverse be my lot.

So help me God.

We've tried our best to help you this far. The rest is up to you. If you can start your new career, you can go forward and succeed!

THE INSIDE TRACK

Who:	Bill Boyd
What:	Paramedic and Fire Captain
Where:	Bellingham Fire Department
	Bellingham, Washington
How long:	Began as an EMT in 1983
Degree:	Paramedic certification; BA degree in Political Science

Insider's Advice

My advice is to finish high school, and complete as much additional schooling as possible. I'm a firm believer in getting a college degree. Take lots of science classes. Especially, you should focus on biology, physiology, and math. Also, get yourself physically fit, and keep it that way to reduce chances of getting back injuries, which are very common. Leadership skills, common sense, a strong sense of compassion, and strong communication skills are extremely important in becoming a successful EMT. If you are in it for the glory, you won't last long, or you will hurt somebody.

Insider's Take on the Future

I am a career firefighter. Our state retirement system is set up so that we don't get the maximum benefits until age 55 and 30 years service. That is what I am shooting for. I was hired at age 25, so it should work out great for me. My plan at this point is to become a battalion chief. I may pursue higher at some point, but we'll see what happens.

APPENDIX A

In addition to contact information for professional associations, this appendix lists national and regional accrediting agencies, job placement services, travel and military organizations, EMT-related unions, and state EMT agencies.

PROFESSIONAL ASSOCIATIONS

Here is a list of professional associations, educational organizations, national and regional accrediting agencies, job placement services, travel and military organizations, and unions that are related to emergency medical technicians and services. You'll also find a list of the state EMT agencies for each state. You may contact them for more information about the EMT profession.

Professional Associations

American Academy of Emergency Medicine
611 E. Wells St.
Milwaukee, WI 53202
800-884-AAEM

American Ambulance Association
3800 Auburn Boulevard, Suite C
Sacramento, CA 95821
916-483-3827

American Nurses Association
600 Maryland Ave. SW
Washington, DC 20024-2571
800-274-4ANA

Associated Public Safety Communications Officers
2040 South Ridgewood
Daytona, FL 32119-8437

EMT Software Inc.
119 N. Commercial St.
Belligham, WA 98225
800-698-1727

International Association of Fire Fighters (IAFF)
1750 New York Ave. NW
Washington, DC 20006
202-737-8484

Manufacturers' Agents National Association
P. O. Box 3467
Laguna Hills, CA 92654-3467

National Association of Emergency Medical Technicians (NAEMT)
102 West Leake St.
Clinton, MS 39056-4252
800-34-NAEMT; 601-924-7744

National Association of EMS Educators
230 McKee Place, Suite 500
Pittsburgh, PA 15213
412-578-3219

National Association of EMS Quality Professionals
3717 Conway Rd.
Orlando, FL 32812
407-281-7396

National Association for Search and Rescue (NASAR)
4500 Southgate Place, Suite 100
Chantilly, VA 20151-1714
703-222-6277

National Collegiate EMS Foundation
P. O. Box 702
Lemont, PA 16851

National EMS Pilot's Association
110 N. Royal St.
Alexandria, VA 22314
888-7NEMSPA; 703-836-8930

National Flight Paramedics Association
7136 S. Yale Rd., Suite 300
Tulsa, OK 74136
800-381-NFPA

National Institute for Urban Search & Rescue
P. O. Box 90909
Santa Barbara, CA 93190
805-569-5066

National League for Nursing
350 Hudson St.
New York, NY 10014
800-669-1656

National Registry of Emergency Medical Technicians (NREMT)
(National Paramedic Society)
6610 Busch Blvd.
Columbus, OH 43229
614-888-4484; 614-888-8920

National Ski Patrol
133 South Van Gordon St., Suite 100
Lakewood, CO 80228
303-988-1111

United States Lifesaving Association
P. O. Box 322
Avon-by-the-Sea, NJ 07717
500-FOR-USLA

Educational Organizations

Accrediting Bureau of Health Education Schools
2700 South Quincy St., Suite 210
Arlington, VA 22206
703-998-1200

Allied Health Education Directory
American Medical Association
P. O. Box 2964
Milwaukee, WI 53201-2964

American Medical Association
Division of Allied Health Education and Accreditation
515 North State Street
Chicago, IL 60610
312-464-5000

Commission on Accreditation of Allied Health Education Programs
515 North State St., Suite 7530
Chicago, IL 60610
312-464-4623

Fellows Memorial Loan Fund
Pensacola Junior College
1000 College Boulevard
Pensacola, FL 32504-8998
904-484-1706
(paramedic training)

Iowa Vocational-Technical Tuition Program
200 Tenth Street, 4th floor
Des Moines, IA 50309-3609

Maryland Higher Education Commission
State Scholarship Administration
16 Francis Street
Annapolis, MD 21401
410-974-5370
(firefighter & rescue squad)

National Association of Health Career Schools
9570 West Pico Blvd., Suite 200
Los Angeles, CA 90035

Police Officer/Firefighter Grant
Illinois Student Assistance Commission
1755 Lake Cook Road
Deerfield, IL 60015-5209

National Accrediting Agencies

Accrediting Commission for Career Schools
and Colleges of Technology (ACCSCT)
Thomas A. Kube, Executive Director
2101 Wilson Boulevard, Suite 302
Arlington, VA 22201
703-247-4212; FAX: 703-247-4533
E-mail: tkube@accsct.org

Accrediting Council for Independent
Colleges and Schools (ACICS)
Stephen D. Parker, Executive Director
750 First Street, NE, Suite 980
Washington, DC 20002-4241
202-336-6780; FAX: 202-842-2593
E-mail: acics@digex.net

Distance Education and Training Council
(DETC)
Michael P. Lambert, Executive Secretary
1601 Eighteenth Street, NW
Washington, DC 20009-2529
202-234-5100; FAX: 202-332-1386
E-mail: detc@detc.org

Regional Accrediting Agencies

Middle States
Middle States Association of Colleges and Schools
Commission on Institutions of Higher Education
3624 Market Street
Philadelphia, PA 19104-2680
215-662-5606; FAX: 215-662-5950
E-mail: jamorse@msache.org

New England States
Charles M. Cook, Director
New England Association of Schools and Colleges
Commission on Institutions of Higher Education
(NEASC-CIHE)
209 Burlington Road
Bedford, MA 07130-1433
617-271-0022; FAX: 617-271-0950
E-mail: ccook@neasc.org

Richard E. Mandeville, Director
New England Association of Schools and Colleges
Commission on Vocational, Technical and Career Institution
(NEASC-CTCI)
209 Burlington Road
Bedford, MA 01730-1433
617-271-0022; FAX: 617-271-0950
E-mail: rmandeville@neasc.org

North Central States

Steve Crow, Executive Director
North Central Association of Colleges and Schools
Commission on Institutions of Higher Education
(NCA)
30 North LaSalle, Suite 2400
Chicago, IL 60602-2504
312-263-0456; FAX: 312-263-7462
E-mail: crow@ncacihe.org

Northwest States

Sandra Elman, Executive Director
Northwest Association of Schools and Colleges
Commission on Colleges
11130 NE 33rd Place, Suite 120
Bellevue, WA 98004
206-827-2005; FAX: 206-827-3395
E-mail: selman@u.washington.edu

Southern States

James T. Rogers, Executive Director
Southern Association of Colleges and Schools
Commission on Colleges (SACS)
1866 Southern Lane
Decatur, GA 30033-4097
404-679-4500; 800-248-7701;
FAX: 404-679-4558
E-mail: jrogers@sacscoc.org

Western States

David B. Wolf, Executive Director
Western Association of Schools and Colleges
Accrediting Commission for Community and Junior Colleges
(WASC-Jr.)
3402 Mendocino Ave.
Santa Rosa, CA 95403-2244
707-569-9177; FAX: 707-569-9179
E-mail: ACCJC@aol.com

Ralph A. Wolff, Executive Director
Western Association of Schools and Colleges
Accrediting Commission for Senior Colleges and Universities
(WASC-Sr.)
c/o Mills College, Box 9990
Oakland, CA 94613-0990
510-632-5000; FAX: 510-632-8361
E-mail: rwolff@wasc.mills.educ

Job Placement Services

American Managed Care & Review Association
1227 25th St. NW, #610
Washington, DC 20037
202-728-0506

American Public Health Association Job Placement Service
1015 15th St. NW
Washington, DC 20005
202-789-5600

American School Health Association Placement Service
P. O. Box 708
Kent, OH 44240
216-245-6296
(federal jobs)

National Association of Personnel Services
3133 Mt. Vernon Ave.
Alexandria, VA 22305

National Association of Temporary Services
119 S. Saint Asaph St.
Alexandria, VA 22314

Travel and Military Organizations

American National Red Cross
National Headquarters
17 and D Streets, NW
Washington, DC 20006

Department of the Air Force Headquarters
U. S. Air Force Recruiting Service (ATC)
Randolph Air Force Base, TX 78150-5421

Department of the Army Headquarters
U. S. Army Recruiting Command
Fort Sheridan, IL 60037-6000

Department of the Coast Guard
Commandant, U. S. Coast Guard
2100 Second Street, SW
Washington, DC 20593
202-267-2229

Department of the Marines
First Marine Corps District Headquarters
605 Stewart Avenue
Garden City, NY 11530-4760
800-MARINES

Department of the Navy
Navy Recruiting Command
4015 Wilson Boulevard
Arlington, VA 22203-1911
800-USA-NAVY

Peace Corps
806 Connecticut Ave., NW
Washington, DC 20525

Project HOPE
Health Sciences Education Center
Carter Hall
Millwood, VA 22646

U. S. Public Health Service Department of Health and Human Services
5600 Fishers Lane, Rm. 17-74
Rockville, MD 20757

World Health Organization
(Pan American Health Organization)
525 23 Street, NW
Washington, DC 20037

EMT-Related Unions

American Federation of State, County, and Municipal Employees
1625 L Street, NW
Washington, DC 20036
202-429-1130

Health Professionals and Allied Employees of New Jersey
110 Kinderkamack Road
Emerson, NJ 07630
201-262-5005

International Association of Fire Fighters
1750 New York Avenue, NW
Washington, DC 20006
202-737-8484

North American EMS Employee Organizations Network (NEEON)
c/o Alan Saly, Secretary
Local 2507 DC 37 AFSCME
299 Broadway, Suite 309
New York, NY 10007
212-385-1152

Service Employees International Union (SEIU)
1313 L Street, NW
Washington, DC 20005
202-898-3333

State EMT Agencies
ALABAMA
Emergency Medical Services Division
Alabama Department of Health
The RSA Tower, 201 Monroe St., Suite 750
Montgomery, AL 36130-3017
334-206-5383

ALASKA
Community Health and Emergency Medical Services Section
Department of Health and Human Services/ Public Health
P. O. Box 110616
Juneau, AK 99811-0616
907-465-3027
Web site: http://www.health.state.ak.us

ARIZONA

Bureau of Emergency Medical Services
Arizona Department of Health Services
1651 E. Morten, Suite 120
Phoenix, AZ 85020
602-255-1170
Web site: http://www.hs.state.az.us

ARKANSAS

Division of Emergency Medical Services and Trauma Systems
Arkansas Department of Health
4815 W. Markham St., Slot 38
Little Rock, AR 72205-3867
501-661-2178
Web site: http://www.doh.state.ar.us

CALIFORNIA

Emergency Medical Services Authority
1930 9th St., Suite 100
Sacramento, CA 95814
916-322-4336
Web site: http://www.emsa.cahwnet.gov

COLORADO

Colorado Department of Health
Emergency Medical Services Division
4300 Cherry Creek Dr. South
Denver, CO 80222
303-692-2980
Web site: http://www.state.co.us/gov_dir/cdphe_dir/em/emhom.htm

CONNECTICUT

Office of Emergency Medical Service
Department of Public Health
410 Capital Ave., MS#12EMS
P. O. Box 340308
Hartford, CT 06134-0308
860-509-7975

DELAWARE

Emergency Medical Services
Blue Hen Corporate Center
655 South Bay Road, Suite 4-H
Dover, DE 19901
302-739-6637

DISTRICT OF COLUMBIA

Emergency Health and Medical Services
800 9th St., SW, 3rd floor
Washington, DC 20024
202-645-5628

FLORIDA

Bureau of Emergency Medical Services
Florida Department of Health
2002-D Old St. Augustine Road
Tallahassee, FL 32301-4881
904-487-1911
Web site: http://www.state.fl.us/health/ems

GEORGIA

Emergency Medical Services
47 Trinity Ave., SW, Suite 104-LOB
Atlanta, GA 30334-5600
404-657-6700
Web site: http://www.dhr.state.ga.us

HAWAII

Emergency Medical Services System
State Department of Health
3627 Kilauea Ave., Room 102
Honolulu, HI 96816
808-733-9210

IDAHO

Emergency Medical Services Bureau
Department of Health and Welfare
3092 Elder Street
Boise, ID 83705
208-334-4000

ILLINOIS

Division of Emergency Medical Services
Illinois Department of Public Health
525 W. Jefferson St.
Springfield, IL 62761
217-785-2080

INDIANA

Indiana Emergency Medical Services Commission
302 W. Washington, Room E208 IGCS
Indianapolis, IN 46204-2258
317-232-3980

IOWA

Emergency Medical Services
Iowa Department of Public Health
Lucas State Office Building
Des Moines, IA 50319-0075
515-281-3239

KANSAS
Board of Emergency Medical Services
109 SW 6th Avenue
Topeka, KS 66603-3826
913-296-7296

KENTUCKY
Emergency Medical Services Branch ·
Department for Health Services
275 E. Main Street
Frankfort, KY 40621
502-564-8963

LOUISIANA
Bureau of Emergency Medical Services
P. O. Box 4215
Baton Rouge, LA 70804
504-342-4881

MAINE
Maine Emergency Medical Services
16 Edison Drive
Augusta, ME 04330
207-287-3953
Web site: http://www.state.me.us/bms/bmshome.html

MARYLAND
Maryland Department of Emergency Medical Services
636 W. Lombard Street
Baltimore, MD 21201-1528
410-706-5074
Web site: http://www.134.192.108.12/home.html

MASSACHUSETTS
Office of Emergency Medical Services
Department of Public Health
470 Atlantic Avenue, 2nd Floor
Boston, MA 02201-2208
617-753-8300

MICHIGAN
Division of Emergency Medical Services
Michigan Department of Consumer and Industry Affairs
P. O. Box 30664
Lansing, MI 48909
517-335-8594

MINNESOTA
Minnesota Emergency Medical Services Regulatory Board
2829 University Avenue, SE, Suite 310
Minneapolis, MN 55414-3222
612-627-6000
Web site: http://www.emsrb.state.mn.us

MISSISSIPPI
Emergency Medical Services
State Department of Health
P. O. Box 1700
Jackson, MS 39215-1700
601-987-3880

MISSOURI
Bureau of Emergency Medical Services
Missouri Department of Health
P. O. Box 570
Jefferson City, MO 65101
573-751-6356

MONTANA

Emergency Medical Services and Injury Prevention Section
Department of Public Health and Human Services
Cogswell Building
P. O. Box 202951
Helena, MT 59620-2951

NEBRASKA

Division of Emergency Medical Services
301 Centennial Mall South, 3rd Floor
Lincoln, NE 68509-5007
402-471-0124

NEVADA

Emergency Medical Services Office
Nevada State Health Division
1550 E. College Parkway, #158
Carson City, NV 89710
702-687-3065

NEW HAMPSHIRE

Bureau of Emergency Medical Services
Health and Welfare Building
6 Hazen Drive
Concord, NH 03301-6527
603-271-4568

NEW JERSEY

New Jersey Department of Health and Senior Services
Office of Emergency Medical Services
CN-360; 50 East State Street, 6th Floor
Trenton, NJ 08625-0360
609-633-7777
Web site: http://www.state.nj.us/health/ems/hlthems.html

NEW MEXICO

Emergency Medical Services Bureau
Department of Health
P. O. Box 26110
Santa Fe, NM 87502-6110

NEW YORK

Bureau of Emergency Medical Services
New York State Health Department
433 River Street, Suite 303
Troy, NY 12180-2299
518-402-0996
Web site: http://www.health.state.ny.us/nysdoh/ems

NORTH CAROLINA

Office of Emergency Medical Services
701 Barbour Drive
P. O. Box 29530
Raleigh, NC 27603
919-733-2285

NORTH DAKOTA

Division of Emergency Health Services
North Dakota Department of Health
600 E. Boulevard Avenue
Bismark, ND 58505-0200
701-328- 2388

OHIO

Ohio Department of Public Safety
Emergency Medical Services
P. O. Box 7167
Columbus, OH 43266-0563
614-466-9447

OKLAHOMA

Emergency Medical Services Division

State Department of Health

1000 NE 10th Street, Room 1104

Oklahoma City, OK 73117-1299

405-271-4027

OREGON

Emergency Medical Services and Systems

Oregon Health Division

800 NE Oregon, Suite 607

Portland, OR 97232

503-731-4011

PENNSYLVANIA

Division of Emergency Medical Services Systems

Pennsylvania Department of Health

P. O. Box 90

Harrisburg, PA 17108

717-787-8741

RHODE ISLAND

Emergency Medical Services Division

Department of Health, Room 404

3 Capitol Hill

Providence, RI 02908-5097

401-277-2401

SOUTH CAROLINA

South Carolina Division of Emergency Medical Services

2600 Bull Street

Columbia, SC 29201

803-737-7204

Web site: http://www.state.sc.us/dhec/hrems.html

SOUTH DAKOTA

Emergency Medical Services Program
Department of Health
445 East Capitol
Pierre, SD 57501
605-773-4779

TENNESSEE

Division of Emergency Medical Services
Department of Health
426 Fifth Avenue, North, 1st Floor, Room 88
Nashville, TN 37247-0701
615-741-2584

TEXAS

Bureau of Emergency Management
Texas Department of Health
1100 49th Street
Austin, TX 78756-3199
512-834-6740
Web site: http://www.tdh.state.tx.us

UTAH

Bureau of Emergency Medical Services
Department of Health
288 N. 1460 West
Box 142852
Salt Lake City, UT 84114-2852
801-538-6435

VERMONT

Emergency Medical Services Division
Department of Health
108 Cherry Street
Box 70
Burlington, VT 05402
802-863-7310

VIRGINIA
Office of Emergency Medical Services
Virginia Department of Health
1538 E. Parham Road
Richmond, VA 23228
804-371-3500
Web site: http://www.vdh.state.ua.us/oems/index.html

WASHINGTON
Department of Health
Office of Emergency Medical and Trauma Prevention
P. O. Box 47853
Olympia, WA 98504-7853
360-705-6745
Web site: http://www.doh.wa.gov/hsqa/emtp

WEST VIRGINIA
West Virginia Office of Emergency Medical Services
1411 Virginia Street, East
Charleston, WV 25301-3013
304-558-3956

WISCONSIN
Emergency Medical Services
Division of Health
P. O. Box 309
Madison, WI 53701-0309
608-266-9781 or 800-793-6820

WYOMING
Emergency Medical Services Program
State of Wyoming
Hathaway Building, Room 527
Cheyenne, WY 82002
307-777-6018

APPENDIX B

Now that you have been through this entire book and know what you need to do to accomplish your goals, look through this appendix for titles that will give you more specific advice on areas with which you need help.

ADDITIONAL RESOURCES

For more information on the topics discussed in this book, refer to the following reading list organized by subject. This list of helpful books is followed by a list of EMT-related periodicals.

BOOKS

Career Guides

Cosgrove, Holli R. *Encyclopedia of Careers and Vocational Guidance.* 10th Ed. Chicago: J.G. Ferguson Pub. 1997.

Dictionary of Occupational Titles. 4th Ed. Vol. 1, 2. Bureau of Labor Statistics. 1991.

Occupational Outlook Handbook. 1996-1997. U. S. Department of Labor.

College Guides

The College Board. *The College Handbook 1998*. 35th Ed. New York: College Entrance Exam Board. 1997.

Peterson's Guide to Two-Year Colleges 1998: The Only Guide to More Than 1,500 Community and Junior Colleges. Princeton: Peterson's. 1997.

Peterson's Vocational and Technical Schools. Princeton: Peterson's Guides. 1994.

The Princeton Review. *The Complete Book of Colleges 1998*. New York: Random House, The Princeton Review. 1997.

Cover Letters

Beatty, Richard H. *The Perfect Cover Letter*. 2nd Ed. New York: John Wiley & Sons. 1997.

Besson, Taunee. *The Wall Street Journal National Business Employment Weekly: Cover Letters*. 2nd Ed. New York: John Wiley & Sons. 1996.

Marler, Patty and Jan Bailey Mattia. *Cover Letters Made Easy*. Lincolnwood, IL: NTC Pub. 1996.

Financial Aid

The College Bluebook: Scholarships, Fellowships, Grants, and Loans. 26th Ed. Education Division. New York: Simon & Schuster. 1997.

College School Service. *College Costs & Financial Aid Handbook*. 18th Ed. New York: The College Entrance Examination Board. 1998.

Davis, Kristen. *Financing College: How To Use Savings, Financial Aid, Scholarships, and Loans to Afford the School of Your Choice*. Washington, DC: Random House. 1996.

Schwartz, John. *College Scholarships and Financial Aid*. 7th Ed. New York: ARCO. 1997.

Some previous edition financial aid guides should also be available at your local library.

Further EMT Reading

Canning, Peter. *Paramedic: On the Front Lines of Medicine*. New York: Ballantine Books. 1997. Real life drama from the experiences of Peter Canning, an EMT-Paramedic.

Sunshine, Linda and John W. Wright. *The Best Hospitals in America*. New York: Gale Research, International Thomson Publishers. 1995.

Interviews

Bloch, Deborah P., Ph.D. *How to Have a Winning Interview*. Illinois: VGM Career Horizons. 1996.

Fry, Ron. *101 Great Answers to the Toughest Interview Questions*. 3rd Ed. Franklin Lakes, NJ: Book-Mart Press. 1996.

Kennedy, Joyce Lain. *Job Interviews for Dummies*. Foster City, CA: IDG Books. 1996.

Yate, Martin John. *Knock 'em Dead with Great Answers to Tough Interview Questions*. Holbrook, MA: Adams Publishing. 1985.

Job Hunting

Bernstein, Sara T. and Kathleen M. Savage, Eds. *Vocational Careers Sourcebook*. New York: Gale Research, International Thomson Publishers. 1996.

Bolles, Richard Nelson. *What Color is Your Parachute?* Ten Speed Press. 1997.

Cubbage, Sue A. and Marcia P. Williams. *The 1996 National Job Hotline Directory*. New York: McGraw-Hill. 1996.

Gilbert, Sara Dulaney. *Internships 1997: The Hotlist for Job Hunters*. 2nd Ed. New York: ARCO. 1997.

Hadley, Joyce. *Where The Jobs Are: The Hottest Careers for the 90's.* 2nd Ed. Hawthorne, NJ: Career Press. 1995.

Job Hunting Made Easy: 20 Simple Steps to Coming Up a Winner. New York: LearningExpress. 1997.

Networking

National Business Employment Weekly. *Networking: Insider's Strategies for Tapping the Hidden Market Where Most Jobs are Found.* New York: John Wiley & Sons, 1994.

Resumes

Adams Resume Almanac & Disc. Holbrook, MA: Adams Media Corporation. 1996.

Haft, Timothy D. *Trashproof Resumes: Your Guide to Cracking the Job Market.* Princeton: Princeton Review, 1995.

Resumes! Resumes! Resumes!: Top Career Experts Show You the Job-Landing Resumes that Sold Them. 3rd Ed. Hawthorne, NJ: Book-Mart Press, Career Press. 1997.

The Guide to Basic Resume Writing. Chicago: VGM Career Horizons, NTC Publishing Group, 1991.

Scholarship Guides

Cassidy, Daniel J. *The Scholarship Book: The Complete Guide to Private-Sector Scholarships, Grants, and Loans for Undergraduates.* Englewood Cliffs, NJ: Prentice Hall. 1996.

Ragins, Marianne. *Winning Scholarships for College: An Insider's Guide.* New York: Henry Holt & Co. 1994.

Scholarships, Grants & Prizes: Guide to College Financial Aid From Private Sources. Princeton: Peterson's Guides. 1998.

Scholarships 1998. New York: Simon & Schuster, Kaplan. 1997.

Some previous edition scholarships guides should also be available at your local library.

Studying

Coman, Marcia J. and Kathy L. Heavers. *How to Improve Your Study Skills*. 2nd Ed. Lincolnwood, IL: NTC Publishing. 1998.

Fry, Ron. *Ron Fry's How To Study Program*. 4th Ed. New Jersey: Career Press. 1996.

How to Study: The Basics Made Easy in 20 Minutes a Day. New York: LearningExpress. 1997.

Read Better, Remember More: The Basics Made Easy in 20 Minutes a Day. New York: LearningExpress. 1997.

Silver, Theodore, M.D., J.D. *The Princeton Review Study Smart: Hands-On Nuts-and-Bolts Techniques for Earning Higher Grades*. New York: Villard Books. 1995.

Test Help

ACT: Powerful Strategies to Help You Score Higher: 1998 Ed. Kaplan. New York: Simon & Schuster. 1997.

ASVAB: Armed Services Vocational Aptitude Battery. New York: LearningExpress. 1997.

EMT Basic Exam: The Complete Preparation Guide. New York: LearningExpress. 1997.

Firefighter Exam: The Complete Preparation Guide. New York: LearningExpress. 1997.

Julihn, Miles and Gail Walraven. *Paramedic Review Guide: Case Studies and Self-Assessment Questions*. Brady Regents: Prentice Hall. 1988.

Katyman, John and Adam Robinson. *Cracking the SAT & PSAT 1998 Edition*. New York: Random House, The Princeton Review. 1997.

Police Officer Exam: The Complete Preparation Guide. New York: LearningExpress, 1997.

Secrets of Taking Any Test: The Basics Made Easy in 20 Minutes a Day. New York: LearningExpress, 1997.

Previous edition SAT and ACT test preparation books should also be available at your local library.

Work Relationships

Bell, Arthur and Smith, Dayle M. *Winning With Difficult People.* New York: Barron's Educational Series, 1991.

Bramson, Robert M., Ph.D. *Coping With Difficult People.* New York: Anchor Press, 1981.

Felder, Leonard. *Does Someone at Work Treat You Badly?* New York: Berkley Books, 1993.

> To order any LearningExpress publication, call toll-free:
> **1–888–551–5627**

PERIODICALS

EMS Magazine
7626 Densmore Ave.
Van Nuys, CA
800-224-4367

Journal of Emergency Medical Services
P. O. Box 2789
Carlsbad, CA 92018
760-431-9797

FIVE WAYS TO MASTER THE BASICS!

IT ISN'T LUCK!

Anyone who wants to get good grades in school, pass entry-level or other job-related exams, or perform well on the job, must master basic skills: Reading Comprehension, Math, Vocabulary and Spelling, Writing, and basic Reasoning Skills.

What's the best way to master these skills?

With LearningExpress **SKILL BUILDERS**! Each book is designed to help you learn the important skills you need in the least amount of time.

Arranged in 20 quick and easy lessons, each guide:

- Pinpoints the areas where you need the most help
- Gives you hundreds of exercises with full answer explanations
- Provides you with tips on scoring your best on school and job-related tests

Skill Builders also feature:

- Specially designed "Before and After" tests to quickly pinpoint strengths, weaknesses *and* chart your progress
- "Skill Building Until Next Time": inventive ways to continue learning on the go

GIVE YOURSELF THE EXCLUSIVE LEARNINGEXPRESS ADVANTAGE!

1. ___	READING COMPREHENSION SUCCESS IN 20 MINUTES A DAY	Item #126-5
2. ___	WRITING SKILLS SUCCESS IN 20 MINUTES A DAY	Item #128-1
3. ___	VOCABULARY/SPELLING SUCCESS IN 20 MINUTES A DAY	Item #127-3
4. ___	PRACTICAL MATH SUCCESS IN 20 MINUTES A DAY	Item #129-X
5. ___	REASONING SKILLS SUCCESS IN 20 MINUTES A DAY	Item #116-8

SPECIFICATIONS: 8 1/2 × 11 • 192-240 PAGES • $15.95 EACH (PAPERBACK)

ORDER THE LEARNINGEXPRESS SKILL BUILDERS YOU NEED TODAY:

Fill in the quantities beside each book and mail your check/money order* for the amount indicated (please include $6.95 postage/handling for the first book and $1.00 for each additional book) to:

LearningExpress, Dept. A040, 20 Academy Street, Norwalk, CT 06850

Or call, TOLL-FREE: **1-888-551-JOBS, Dept. A040,** to place a credit card order.

Also available in your local bookstores

Please allow at least 2-4 weeks for delivery. Prices subject to change without notice   *NY, CT, & MD residents add appropriate sales tax

Order Form

CALIFORNIA EXAMS
- ___ @ $35.00   CA Police Officer
- ___ @ $35.00   CA State Police
- ___ @ $35.00   CA Corrections Officer
- ___ @ $20.00   CA Law Enforcement Career Guide
- ___ @ $35.00   CA Firefighter
- ___ @ $30.00   CA Postal Worker
- ___ @ $35.00   CA Allied Health

NEW JERSEY EXAMS
- ___ @ $35.00   NJ Police Officer
- ___ @ $35.00   NJ State Police
- ___ @ $35.00   NJ Corrections Officer
- ___ @ $20.00   NJ Law Enforcement Career Guide
- ___ @ $35.00   NJ Firefighter
- ___ @ $30.00   NJ Postal Worker
- ___ @ $35.00   NJ Allied Health

TEXAS EXAMS
- ___ @ $35.00   TX Police Officer
- ___ @ $30.00   TX State Police
- ___ @ $35.00   TX Corrections Officer
- ___ @ $20.00   TX Law Enforcement Career Guide
- ___ @ $35.00   TX Firefighter
- ___ @ $30.00   TX Postal Worker
- ___ @ $32.50   TX Allied Health

NEW YORK EXAMS
- ___ @ $30.00   NYC/Nassau County Police Officer
- ___ @ $30.00   Suffolk County Police Officer
- ___ @ $30.00   New York City Firefighter
- ___ @ $35.00   NY State Police
- ___ @ $35.00   NY Corrections Officer
- ___ @ $20.00   NY Law Enforcement Career Guide
- ___ @ $35.00   NY Firefighter
- ___ @ $30.00   NY Postal Worker
- ___ @ $35.00   NY Allied Health
- ___ @ $30.00   NY Postal Worker

MASSACHUSETTS EXAMS
- ___ @ $30.00   MA Police Officer
- ___ @ $30.00   MA State Police Exam
- ___ @ $30.00   MA Allied Health

FLORIDA EXAMS
- ___ @ $35.00   FL Police Officer
- ___ @ $35.00   FL Corrections Officer
- ___ @ $20.00   FL Law Enforcement Career Guide
- ___ @ $30.00   FL Postal Worker
- ___ @ $32.50   FL Allied Health

ILLINOIS EXAMS
- ___ @ $25.00   Chicago Police Officer
- ___ @ $25.00   Illinois Allied Health

The MIDWEST EXAMS
(Illinois, Indiana, Michigan, Minnesota, Ohio, and Wisconsin)
- ___ @ $30.00   Midwest Police Officer Exam
- ___ @ $30.00   Midwest Firefighter Exam

The SOUTH EXAMS
(Alabama, Arkansas, Georgia, Louisiana, Mississippi, North Carolina, South Carolina, and Virginia)
- ___ @ $25.00   The South Police Officer Exam
- ___ @ $25.00   The South Firefighter Exam

NATIONAL EDITIONS
- ___ @ $14.95   ASVAB (Armed Services Vocational Aptitude Battery)
- ___ @ $12.95   U.S. Postal Worker Exam
- ___ @ $15.00   Federal Clerical Worker Exam
- ___ @ $12.95   Bus Operator Exam
- ___ @ $12.95   Sanitation Worker Exam
- ___ @ $20.00   Allied Health Entrance Exams

NATIONAL CERTIFICATION EXAM
- ___ @ $20.00   Home Health Aide Certification Exa
- ___ @ $20.00   Nursing Assistant Certification Exam
- ___ @ $20.00   EMT-Basic Certification Exam

CAREER STARTERS
- ___ @ $14.95   Computer Technician
- ___ @ $14.95   Health Care
- ___ @ $14.95   Paralegal
- ___ @ $14.95   Administrative Assistant/Secretary
- ___ @ $14.00   Civil Service

To Order, Call TOLL-FREE: 1-888-551-JOBS, Dept. A040

Or, mail this order form with your check or money order* to:
LearningExpress, Dept. A040, 20 Academy Street, Norwalk, CT 06850

Please allow at least 2-4 weeks for delivery. Prices subject to change without notice   *NY, CT, & MD residents add appropriate sales tax

 LEARNINGEXPRESS

An Affiliate Company of Random House, Inc.